$29.95

Come and Get It!

Come and Get It!

The Saga of Western Dinnerware

Corinne Joy Brown

Johnson Books Boulder

Copyright © 2011 by Corinne Joy Brown

All rights reserved.
No part of this publication may be reproduced or transmitted in any form or by any means, electronic or mechanical, including photocopy, recording, or any information storage and retrieval system, without permission in writing from the publisher.

Published by Johnson Books, a Big Earth Publishing company
3360 Mitchell Lane, Suite E, Boulder, Colorado 80301
1-800-258-5830
E-mail: books@bigearthpublishing.com
www.bigearthpublishing.com

Some of the quotes in this book are from *Never Ask a Man the Size of His Spread* by Gladiola Montana.
Reprinted with permission from Gibbs Smith, Publisher.

All photos taken by the author from her collection unless otherwise noted.
Cover and text design by Rebecca Finkel

9 8 7 6 5 4 3 2 1

Library of Congress Cataloging-in-Publication Data
Brown, Corinne Joy, 1948-
Come and get it! : the saga of Western dinnerware / Corinne Joy Brown.
p. cm.
ISBN 978-1-55566-439-8
1. Ceramic tableware—United States—History—20th century.
2. Decoration and ornament, Rustic—West (U.S.)
3. Cowboys—Collectibles—West (U.S.) 4. West (U.S.)—Collectibles.
I. Title.
NK4695.T33B76 2010
738.3'7—dc22 2010000216

Printed in China by Hing Yip Printing Co., Ltd.

Contents

Yesterday and Today

In the Beginning

Many have asked how this book came about. In fact, I often ask myself. As with most writers, the written word is our way of processing how we feel about an experience; it's how we understand discovery or change. This book was a direct result

Restaurant ware circa 1960. Back stamp reads "Mayer China Made Expressly for RH Supply, Fort Lauderdale, FLA." on the cup and saucer, and "Jackson China of Falls Creek, Pennsylvania" on the steak platter, bouillon cup, and salad plate. A perfect choice for any Western hotel or dining room.

of my newfound passion for collecting Western-themed china and tableware. To me, it was inevitable. I needed to record my journey as each new acquisition added an important piece to an intriguing puzzle.

Collecting is a highly personal activity. In the case of dinnerware, I've learned that some enthusiasts only seek items by a certain manufacturer, often a single pattern or style, enabling them to complete an entire collection, from full place settings to accessories. Others prefer to hunt down a certain era, or color, like red ruby glass or white ironstone.

My goal, however, was to obtain just enough of a single product by any manufacturer who used Western imagery

Top: Large plate, reproduction of Wallace China "Rodeo" pattern, produced by True West Home. Small salad plate is a vintage original by Wallace, 1940s. Artist Till Goodan.
Left: True West Home Christmas pattern, artwork by Till Goodan.

so I could assess the variety of interpretation and approach. That might sound disconnected, like no framework at all, but in fact I am most intrigued by change, how an idea sustains and evolves.

Not every pattern with a Western theme has qualified for my collection. I've been selective. For me, a worthy piece of china isn't just about a particular motif or decoration. As a former art teacher who has studied both art history and ceramics, I'm sensitive to what defines a successful product—one where the relationship of decoration to shape must fully agree. I've looked at every piece I came across and asked myself if the maker was attempting a new interpretation in the spirit of the time, or evoking an old idea in a new way.

As a result, I've selected those examples that seemed chronologically significant, aesthetically pleasing, and well made. New surprises seem to show up daily. I've looked for quality production, surface decoration applied with integrity and forethought, and products I feel have staying power, not just promotional items or commercial efforts.

I found myself interested in all aspects of design: hand-painted, transfer or decal ware, as well as stamped, embossed, and airbrushed designs. I've even added collector's plates bearing all types of Western subjects.

A romantic series, "El Rancho" by Wallace China, depicting Monument Valley, a frontier town, and a lonesome traveler, circa 1950.

Canyonlands view, Monument Valley—a sacred and iconic place to many who love the West. (Courtesy Nathan La Font, San Juan County, Utah, Visitor Services)

Once You're Hooked . . .

My very first introduction to Western dinnerware began just a few years ago with a writing assignment on tableware manufacturers for *Western & English Today*, a magazine that serves the Western retail market. The research for that story opened a door to a world I found both curious and attractive. In particular, one of the producers I contacted was True West Home, the current manufacturer of vintage dinnerware from a company known as Wallace China of California that ceased production in 1963. Wallace had created a collection called "Westward Ho" with four different series, and True West Home was once again using the very same designs of the original artist, Till Goodan. I reveled in its brilliance, quality, and charm.

As I considered True West's history, I deduced that if there was one vintage producer then there had to be others, and so the search began. After weeks of perusing local antique dealers in Denver and getting acquainted with online auction houses, I discovered an intriguing oval serving platter with an illustration of Monument Valley on its face. It was made by Wallace China, too. This pattern was a key design in what was called the "El Rancho" series, a restaurant ware produced in the 1950s. For me, that discovery was the turning point.

I was hooked. The platter touched me, evoking a deep emotional response. The image was drawn from the actual location on the Utah-Colorado border, a breathtaking landscape that was once the location of dozens of Western films, especially those made by award-winning filmmaker John Ford.

Yes, that's actually me, once upon a time, perched on top of a stuffed horse, circa 1951.

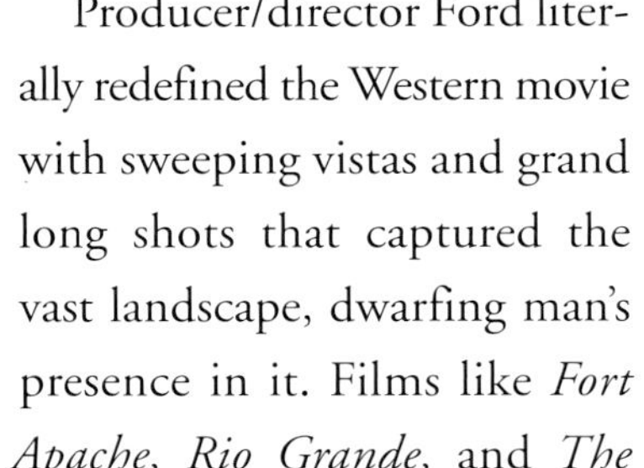

Producer/director Ford literally redefined the Western movie with sweeping vistas and grand long shots that captured the vast landscape, dwarfing man's presence in it. Films like *Fort Apache, Rio Grande,* and *The Searchers* filled my youth with dreams of cowboys and the frontier West. Passing my childhood in the 1950s and adolescence in the 1960s, my youth was not unlike so many others who grew up at the height of Western film and the birth of the TV Western. It seemed uncanny that this iconic scene, complete with a cowboy and his chuck wagon under a big Western sky, could have been drawn and reproduced on a plate.

Like others of my era, I had practically been weaned on legendary Hollywood Western heroes. The captivating line-up, including Hopalong Cassidy, Roy Rogers, and the Lone Ranger, were steady fare, and on most Saturday mornings I watched programs like *Annie Oakley, Sky King,* and *My Friend Flicka.* I knew that when I grew up I would be a cowgirl. At least I hoped I would.

I stayed with those Westerns right through high school, when the Cartwright brothers on *Bonanza* turned the Western into a family relationship. My first real crush was on a TV series character named Rowdy Yates from *Rawhide* (Clint Eastwood). Actor James Arness from *Gunsmoke* taught me respect for the law, and programs like *Maverick, Have Gun Will Travel,* and *Wagon Train* were all weekly favorites. By the time I was in college, *Dr. Quinn Medicine Woman* had replaced our gritty Western hero with a female, and I adored her, too.

"Art is the chief means of breaking bread with the dead."

—W.H. Auden

Eventually, the formula TV Western was replaced by cops and robbers, and the struggle between good and evil came from our city streets. For yet another decade, only the big screen would continue to re-format the cowboy in a series of roles to lure a new audience, but the bounty of those golden years would never come back again. Gone were those impeccable guys in the white hats, the handsome singing cowboys, and the fearless men who brought justice, law, and order to the Wild West.

From There to Here

That hero-laden childhood and uniquely American adolescence prepared me for a relentless case of nostalgia that, in part, helped fuel this book. In addition, there's the vantage point of age. At this point in time, I can see it all too clearly. Nostalgia is a funny thing—the older we are, the better it gets. It's an excuse to reminisce, and doing so justifies a longing for the past.

I'm proud to admit that way back then I actually owned a Roy Rogers lunch box, a red suede fringed cowgirl outfit, and a pair of black Justin boots with turquoise stitching that sat on the floor by my bed until I outgrew them. I received my first horse when I was seven years old and rode him through high school. I read *Smokey the Cowhorse* by Will James at least a dozen times, owned a hand-tooled Western saddle (and still do), wore a striped woolen Pendleton jacket, front-button Levis, and competed in the National Western Stock Show through my teens, but I never saw a Western image on a dinner plate until the year 2007.

"How in the world did I miss that?" I wondered when I first saw it.

I couldn't even imagine such a thing existed. My European mother certainly never bought one. We ate off 1950s Melamine in the kitchen and fine china in the dining room. So, since I couldn't go back and live my life all over again, I decided to bring this book and all its images to you because just maybe you missed it, too. Or perhaps, just seeing all this Western ware for the first time will fill you with joy and wonder, just as it did for me.

Restaurant ware by Jackson China, Falls Creek, Pennsylvania. Simple brand design with air brushed rim, circa 1950s.

Acknowledgments

Special thanks go to a number of individuals who helped make the production of this book special in so many ways:

To Wil Garcia, former owner/partner of Hooked on Glass in Denver, who nurtured my curiosity and love for vintage dinnerware by answering all my questions and sharing his library and wonderful shop. To Pat Turner at True West Home who first sent me the amazing book on the history of china and glass and so encouraged this effort. Thanks, too, go to Betty Andrews Goodan, daughter of artist Till Goodan, who shared her father's work with me and who maintains his vision, integrity, and brilliance in her alliance with True West Home and manufacturer H.F. Coors China. Together they have given Till Goodan's dinnerware designs new life. And to Dirck Schou at H.F. Coors China Company for an inside look at the manufacturing process.

To Chuck Rand, Dickinson Research Center Director, National Cowboy and Western Heritage Museum in Oklahoma City for patiently answering many questions and supplying me with resource material from the Museum's collection. And to Don Reeves, Curator of Cowboy Culture at the Museum, for his special help in clarifying some of my content with his expertise. To Colleen Hudson of the Dude Ranch Association, and Dave Folckemer of the Royal China Collectors Club.

To Robert K. Newman, The Old Print Shop, Inc., New York City, for procuring the image by Currier and Ives. To Cheryl Rogers Barnett, daughter of Roy Rogers and Dale Evans, for help in tracking down the dinnerware made for the Roy Rogers Museum. Also to Elizabeth

Hand-carved leather notebook cover by Silver King Silversmiths, Chatsworth, CA.

Pink of Dallas, Texas, for her great memories of yesteryear, and Mr. Robert Warren of Frisco, Texas, for introducing me to her.

Appreciation goes to Lisa Conklin at Replacements Ltd., an astounding source for consumers who need to replace or add onto existing china, and to Robert Goins, Collectibles Specialist there. To Julie Rose for her accessories, and to Jet Zarkadas, Los Griegos Studio, Santa Fe, and Paul Harbaugh of Denver, both for their help with dude ranches.

To San Juan County Economic Development and Visitor Services and photographer Nathan La Font. To artist Tandi Venter and Encore Art Group; to Tim O'Byrne, Editor of *Working Ranch* magazine; and Fran Smith of *Western Horseman.* To Museum Director Tricia Dixon, National Cowgirl Museum, Fort Worth, Texas, and to Billie Frank, 7L Ranch, the ultimate cowgirl. To Bob Anderson at *Trail Dust* magazine for his generosity and expertise on Western film and his collection of vintage images, and to Jeff Hildebrandt of the Westerns Channel, Starz Entertainment. To Fred Goodwin and Concept Productions, Western memorabilia specialist, for his loan of material and support. To Trent Johnson of Greeley Hat Works; Jennifer Dubberly for Justin Boots; Vicky and Parley Pearce of Hamley Saddles & Western Emporium; and Tom Baldwin, custom spur maker.

To Judy Wagner at Montana Silversmiths (Lifestyles); Abigail Minckler of WesternWare; Steve Weil of Rockmount Ranch Wear; Marsha Roth and Jim Ralph at Stillmeadow Pottery; Kim and Thom Norby at Norby Studios Ltd.; Joe Ragosta and Kandy Steeples at Frankoma Pottery; Carol O'Connell at Rivers Edge Products; Jacqueline Smiley at Vintage Revival; Skip Browning at Hartstone Pottery; Dave Shannon at Carlisle Food Service; Dave Conley at the Homer Laughlin Company; Jenny Dubberly at French | West | Vaughan; Jacki Schtuff at Restaurantware Collectors.com; artists Lynn Brown and Paul Cameron Smith; Marty and Heather Roberts of Cowboy Living; Goldie and Buck Taylor; Buckeye, Teal, and Tona Blake; Kathy Kindig at Pipestone; John Comstock at Western Sizzlin'; Carl Culham at the Pendleton Round Up; Kelly Holly Shev at Pendleton Home Company; Gene Adler at Gibson USA; Sheryl Randolph at Ponderosa/Bonanza Steakhouses; Jasmina Grbic at Vandor LLC; Skip Browning at Hartstone Pottery; Adam Jahiel, Tabitha Smith, Michael Gamer and David Stoeklein, photographers.

Warmest thanks are owed to Janet Hix of Texas, the consummate collector and a china authority in her own right, without whose encouragement and extra photos this book would have have been so much less.

To Lindsay Allen, my "accidental" assistant, who showed up in the nick of time and helped coax this book to life. Her patience, follow through, and steady hand on the camera made her a joy to work with. To my patient husband who lived with dinnerware and props throughout the house for a whole summer. To all the other countless folks who advised, sold china, or referred me in the right direction, I thank you, too. And most of all, thanks to Mira Perrizo of Johnson Books, for seeing the vision and accepting this project to share with other dinnerware collectors everywhere. Some things are just meant to be.

CHAPTER 1

Introduction

Is it Art or is it Kitsch?

Dinnerware as a Collectible?

There are some who might doubt the justification of a book extolling the virtues of a mass-produced item made originally for everyday use. For most people, dinnerware sets are rarely considered lifetime acquisitions or investments. They're simply used until the number of plates left no longer serves a family's needs. A trip to any Goodwill store or donation center will reveal thousands of pieces of plateware, unmatched and unwanted—the detritus of a generation.

Finer sets of china, usually more complete, are often retained and passed onto one's children to become heirlooms destined for the next generation. Unwanted collections end up in antique stores or at dinnerware emporiums like Replacements Ltd., a repository for almost every make and brand. This is the place where you can sell what you have or buy what you need. (Also where to go when you break your mother's best soup bowl. With luck, they'll have one like it.)

But everyday pottery and stoneware, the stuff of discount and department stores, was, after all, created to seduce, entice, and lure the consumer for the short run.

Table display of porcelain products made by Cowboy Living using "Barbwire" and "Classic West" patterns. Original watercolor images by artist Eve Armson. A ranch breakfast to be proud of.

Patterns were, and still are, dictated by popular home fashion trends, color forecasts, or promotions around a season or theme. Collections come and go—one year's hottest pattern might be the next year's dud.

To better understand this ebb and flow, I went to the "Popular Culture" website, authored by T.V. Reed, who is a professor of American Studies at Washington State University, where he teaches a course in American Popular Culture. He points out that "no analysis of popular culture is complete unless it sees that culture in the wider determining context of a general political economy. Whatever else popular culture may be, it's deeply embedded in capitalist, for-profit mass production." That of course, includes the making of china and glassware.

Many factors affect production of utilitarian goods. Reed also points out that the values attached to mass culture reflect the class values of the producers of that culture. Values often limit product content, marginalizing the viewpoints of individuals and groups that are not part of the mostly white, mostly male, mostly upper-middle to upper-class folks who generally control the production of popular culture.

One might wonder how most mass-market products, diverse as they are, cross social strata as well as they do. But in our material society, where people spend lifetimes collecting things, products themselves are powerful links to status, heritage, place, and experience. If a dinnerware set is featured in an upscale catalog, then some as-

Another version of "El Rancho" pattern china, produced after the Wallace China Company was taken over by Shenango China in the 1960s. This version has no center decal. (Photo by Lindsay Allen)

sume that acquisition grants identity. Buy the goods and be perceived as a person with good taste.

In addition, various constraints in the process of production shape content. The all-important need to make a profit shapes both the product and how popular culture accepts it. In the case of dinnerware, the high costs of hand finishing, packaging, and shipping all create limitations based on which pieces are developed, rejected, or refined. Every factor weighs in when choosing the kind of clay body, the type of surface decoration, the durability, and the aesthetics. The end result is a highly deliberate decision tied to profit.

In these difficult times, when the global economy provides for lower cost goods to be produced offshore rather than in America, more and more manufacturers are turning to cheap labor in China, Japan, Korea, and the Philippines. But in spite of the economic advantage of such a move, some dinnerware is still being produced on American soil, carrying on a proud tradition.

In the world of restaurant ware, where replacement costs are paramount, themed or decorated china is no longer seen by many as a smart choice. The expense of replacement is considerable. Author Barbara Conroy points out in her encyclopedic book, *Restaurant China Volume II,* that "[approximately] 80 percent of today's commercial ware is plain or embossed white. In comparison to the late 1930s through the 1960s, custom designs are seldom ordered. Long gone are the days of deep tan, blue, pink, and yellow china bodies."

But there once was a time when that wasn't the case. Logos, emblems, and colorful china were the norm. The West as a decorative theme especially has ebbed and flowed in the national psyche, as well as in the marketplace. It was once a powerful and much loved decorating motif that sold to cafes, diners, restaurants, and hotel dining rooms. Out of favor in most of those venues, it's now making its comeback on the home front.

But just what gives this theme its staying power? And how did it become so popular in the first place, and why?

The following pages will explore some of the answers. Time has a remarkable way of changing what was once deemed kitsch into that which is of value. After all, popular taste is both fickle and shallow. Yesterday's castaways can truly become tomorrow's collectibles. We all know that in America the thirst for the new drives an ever-changing surplus of products to our door (these days, to our desk via the Internet), but the real challenge for the consumer is to search for what has meaning and personal value. Considering its current demand, Western-themed dinnerware, made yesterday or today, appears to have both for a growing number of collectors.

About this Book's Design

Since the 1960s, the kitchen has slowly become the center of modern day domestic life, a showplace for personal tastes and style. I like to think of the dining table as its stage. China, flatware, and even glassware speak for our preferences for tradition and the past, for the cutting edge and the new, and an appreciation of the moment.

Dinnerware patterns, placemats, table linens, drapery, and upholstery fabrics all express the influences of the day. For the sake of reference and context, the many textile samples included in this book were selected to complement the dinnerware from each era.

CHAPTER 2

"I Can See by Your Dinnerware that You are a Cowboy"

This example of the once popular Monterrey Ware was a frequent giveaway or premium that included a mug and a cereal bowl. Made in Mexico in the old style with a scene of the cow camp cook at work. Highly collectible and still in use at some dude ranches. Circa 1960.

Make no mistake, most Western-themed dinnerware has been produced by someone who never met a cowboy or sat on the back of a horse. After all, manufacturing is a business. Only a handful of Western dinnerware producers, back in the heyday or today, were or are connected to the product or lifestyle they espouse—they don't live on ranches. But those few producers and artists that do have an obvious edge—their dinnerware seems to have a certain authenticity.

Western tableware, however, does have a legitimate heritage. It's rich with symbol and story and, in my mind, has a traceable origin. And you don't have to look too far back to find it.

When Cowboys Rode the Open Range

In the latter half of the nineteenth century, when working cowboys herded cattle across open country and up and down trails from Texas to Montana, survival depended on a fully equipped chuck wagon. As they followed their herds, they brought along a uniquely adapted traveling kitchen that doled out meals to a hungry crew. To a cowboy, the chuck wagon chef, who was camp cook (and often doctor, too) was second only to the trail boss in importance.

Cowboys assemble for an evening meal before the chuck wagon, circa 1880s. (Courtesy Wild West vintage photos)

In those days, crockery, or plates made of clay, was unheard of on the trail. Instead, metal—mostly tin—plates were the standard. Coffee, and lots of it, was brewed up fresh and served out of enameled steel coffee pots and tin cups. These accoutrements could be cleaned with water from a stream or scoured out with sand. Either way, the plates were invincible, as well as stackable, and easy to pack away into the chuck wagon with the cooking utensils. Manufacturers later added decorative enamel to the surface of plates to make cleaning easier and add color and pattern to the plain metal dishware (a product known as graniteware or enamelware), a choice that became synonymous with cowboy life. It became so popular, it's still in demand and production today.

The problem with graniteware was the occasional chipping of the enamel, especially on the edges, a feature that didn't actually affect performance but showed wear and tear. In many ways, that just added character and uniqueness to each plate.

Stoneware, earthenware, and porcelain dinnerware certainly had their place. Fine sets were imported from England and France for the well-to-do who lived in cities and could afford such luxuries. But thanks to the transcontinental railroad, settlers on the Frontier West could set a nice table, too. Goods of all kinds crisscrossed the plains, and women who dreamed of fine china could have it by accessing catalog companies like Sears and Roebuck that sold everything from saddles to

Plain or decorated, ironstone was everybody's reliable service at the turn of the nineteenth century. The wash basin and pitcher might have graced a lady's vanity. Circa 1920–30s. (Courtesy Hampden Antique Market, Denver, CO, Proprietor John Helke, photo by the author)

soup tureens. The ease with which a product was shipped to even the most remote places allowed that the tables of sodbusters and cattlemen alike could be graced with decent pottery.

One of the many widely used imports, ironstone china, was first created in England in 1813 and imported to America in the 1840s and '50s. It became a popular tableware, especially in rural farming communities, where it was often referred to as "thrasher's ware." It was made of an improved china body, harder than earthenware and stronger than porcelain, often with decorative transfer patterns or hand-brushed designs. According to the Ironstone China Association, these dinner, tea, and chamber sets were often embossed with three-dimensional designs featuring wheat, prairie flowers, or corn sheaves to please the many farming families who used them during harvest festivals and other feasts.

Archival photos show these dishes in one form or another used in logging camps, gold camps, and a variety of schools and institutions across the West, a predecessor in kind to the sturdy tableware to come out of America's own flourishing potteries during the early 1900s.

According to Ernie and Bev Dieringer, members of the White Ironstone China Association, "Ironstone is recorded as the china most often taken west, or shipped to cities like St. Louis from where it was then distributed farther on. Most often, it was a white clear-glazed earthenware, so durable it could withstand shipping by covered wagon. Some sets were sent by steamship up the Missouri River to the pioneer areas of the Northwest. Two of those paddlewheel steamships, the *Arabia* and the *Bertrand,* sank in the 1800s and their cargo has been salvaged and is now on display. The *Arabia*'s contents, carefully contained in a museum in Kansas City, Missouri, yielded a huge amount of ironstone china intended for pioneer towns, settlements, ranchers, farmers, and miners. We've even seen photos of pioneer mud huts in Nebraska with ironstone inside."

Ironstone was often decorated with engraved designs in blue, mulberry, and polychrome colors, some of which were made to flow or bleed, which intentionally blurred the designs. "White Ironstone" and "Flow Blue" were, and still appear to be, the most popular.

CHAPTER 3

Form Follows Function

Dinnerware and Food

It's inconceivable to write a book about any kind of dinnerware without acknowledging the importance of food. China, porcelain, stoneware, plastic, and even paper dishes were all created to enable humankind to eat. Tempting though it was, space limitations here meant leaving the recipes and the cooking of Western cuisine to cookbook writers and food historians, another challenge entirely.

But food is, after all, why special dishes call for their own unique preparation and presentation. Hence the various kinds of serving plates, soup bowls, gravy boats, soup tureens, relish trays, coffee carafes, dessert plates, butter pat dishes, and more. The need for specific crockery grew around a nation's passion for food, and Western dinnerware—a mid-twentieth-century creation—was no exception.

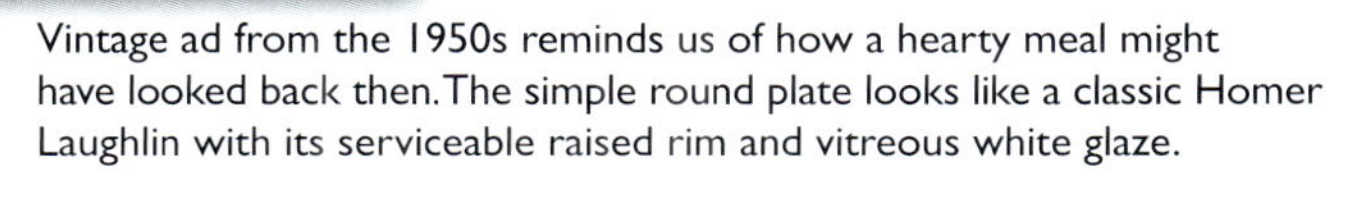

Vintage ad from the 1950s reminds us of how a hearty meal might have looked back then. The simple round plate looks like a classic Homer Laughlin with its serviceable raised rim and vitreous white glaze.

It's important to note that for years the major consumers of Western dinnerware were the restaurant and hotel industries. Back in its nascence, restaurants, dude ranches, and various eateries catered to the appetites of a different America, one whose customers sat down to the table or counter with no holds barred, a time long before calorie- or carbohydrate-conscious menus.

Back then, before fast food, drive-ins, and convenience packaging, restaurant meals across the West were chef-prepared. Breakfasts included American classics like steak and eggs, hash browns, grits, and pancakes. Lunch and dinner might include fried chicken, hams, stews, and roasts, mashed potatoes and gravy, and plenty of side dishes. Fruit cups, bouillion bowls, relish platters, and bread baskets were standard. Homemade biscuits, rolls, cakes, and pies were the additional offerings of simple counter service or a great table. In turn, hefty serving platters and side plates were needed to bring these meals to the customer. Beverages required a variety of coffee urns, pitchers, and creamers, and a legion of demitasse, six-ounce, eight-ounce, and even ten-ounce mugs and cups. The variety of china produced to fill the need was staggering.

Common to all the commercial dinnerware in the mid-1900s, as well as now, was the need for durability: tableware that was thick, heavy, chip-resistant, ovenproof, and dishwasher safe—quality dishes with the ability to perform and survive. Dense, hardworking stoneware or heavy commercial porcelain service was, and still is, the norm. Food simply stayed hot longer

If you can remember drinking coffee years ago out of a heavy porcelain cup with bold cattle brands around the rim, you might be one of the many who swear that the coffee tasted richer back then than at any other time. Or maybe that wonderful old cowboy cup by Wallace China of California just made it seem that way.

Above: Surely there's no better use for this generous platter by Frankoma than a fresh hot quesadilla. The beautiful glaze color added just what I wanted to this favorite appetizer. From their current collection of "Ranch" dinnerware.

Below: Combining vintage plates with new ones is a great way of entertaining. This informal breakfast table features Cowboy Living's "Barbwire" and "Classic West" collections, along with their "Buckaroo" stoneware and Frankoma's "Wagon Wheel" salt and pepper shakers. Center pieces are a vintage McCoy coffee pot and covered wagon food server.

and could be served in a way that was inviting and practical.

Although dining preferences and food trends may have changed, the need to present an appetizing meal on an attractive and presentable plate hasn't. It's no wonder that many of the patterns manufactured for restaurant use, such as the vintage china made by the Wallace, Tepco, Homer Laughlin, Sterling, or Syracuse companies, found their way into consumers' hands—not for collectible or decorative purposes, but for everyday use. In some circles, it's considered very chic these days to use vintage restaurant ware. Thank Martha Stewart for the freedom to mix vintage with flea market with everyday china and set tables to remember. She did, made it look wonderful, and opened the door to eclectic dining, allowing the past and present to merge.

"Forsaking hearth and home and throwing in with the great Overland Migration, weary pioneers struggled westward in record numbers during the peak years of the Overland Crossing, 1840–1919, seeking reassurance where they could, and comfort when possible. Some hymned, others hewed, but nearly all were in accord when it came to the delights of plain cooking, as remembered from home."

—**Cathy Lucetti,** *Home on the Range: A Culinary History of the American West*

CHAPTER 4

The Roots of Western Dinnerware

This dinner plate features cowboys gathered around the fire. It's a miniature masterpiece by artist Paul Davidson for the famed "Winchester '73" series produced by Vernon Kilns. All pieces are hand painted under the glaze.

So just precisely when did dinnerware manufacturers begin to decorate our tables with the illustrated West? One can't pinpoint the exact year, but rather the era and the conditions. According to the archival publication *China and Glass in America 1880–1980: From Table Top to TV Tray,* organized in 2001 by the Dallas Museum of Art and former curator Charles L. Venable to accompany the exhibition of the same name, "the 1940s and '50s were ripe for a new expression of casual dining."

Following the end of World War II and the reunification of American families, a move to the suburbs defined the growth of many urban areas. With that came a commitment to family and neighborhood as Americans entered a time of renewed prosperity and hope, steeped in post-war optimism.

Venable points out that residential architecture ushered in a new style of inexpensive family housing inspired by southern California patio homes, referred to as a "ranch." Here, an open flow and spacious continuum made living on one level practical and functional. Cathedral, or open, angled ceilings allowed for skylights and clerestory windows, creating a new modern feel. The idea of flow was more important than privacy. Most of all, kitchens were designed to be integrated, without walls closing them off, allowing for a new, more casual way of entertaining where the dinner guest could actually chat with the host and serve him or herself—a novel idea.

In addition, the buffet-serving concept had arrived, where dishes were displayed and people helped themselves, along with informal cocktail parties and neighborhood get-togethers on the patio, often followed by outdoor dining.

The charm and popularity of eating outside captured every manufacturer's heart, especially with the invention of the most important lure ever manufactured to draw men and boys into the fray—the freestanding portable barbecue grill.

Many homes had outside cooking grills long before the 1950s, but these were usually built-in or attached to the side of the house. The use of a fire made of charcoal that could be contained and wheeled anywhere in the yard was a new means by which fathers and sons could join in an age-old bond of food preparation.

"So deep was the male-bonding reference in fact," said Venable, "that in the beginning all charcoal grilling, the utensils, oversized and intimidating in design, as well as aprons and other cooking accessories, were gender specific—they were created for men, elevating the act of cooking outdoors into a respectable, primal act."

Earlier, in another far-off time, in a very different kind of setting, men also sat around a fire to eat and commune. Cowboys, cooking out on the range, with nothing but the starry sky above as their roof and the crackle of flames before them, shared the same bond.

Divided grill plate made in Japan, circa 1950s.
Glaze highly cracked but otherwise a perfect survivor.

Imagine finding this postcard on a trip West back in the 1940s. It's not dated, but the card says, "A scene typical of the old days on the Western range." The postage is a two-cent stamp.

Producers in Hollywood had immortalized this scene in countless ways. Almost every good Western had one, and the endearing chuck wagon cook was often a standard secondary character.

In response to this new American outdoor leisure activity, dinnerware manufacturers rose to the call. By 1950, California producers Vernon Kilns and Wallace China, and a few years later Shenango Pottery and the Homer Laughlin Company of Ohio, had portrayed this evocative scene in all its detail. Those early patterns were masterpieces of illustration, comprehensive, carefully drawn and considered, with transfer images designed to fit each and every plate, creamer, or platter. Many were hand colored under the glaze. Full of artistry, they told a remarkable story. The cowboy camp and chuck wagon supper had come home.

"Western Round-Up" Ranch Ware by Shenango. Steak platter depicting cowboys gathered around the chuck wagon, circa 1950s–1960s.

CHAPTER 5

"Head 'Em Off at the Pass ..."

From Tabletop to Movie Screen and Back Again

The tableware industry of the twentieth century, as today, was a response to consumer interests. There are many, therefore, who believe that the popularity of Western dinnerware foremost mirrored America's fascination with the Western movie, one of the longest running film genres in cinematic history.

In part, that might be true. For during the golden years of this remarkable era, from the 1930s through the 1960s, a steady stream of big screen and B Western movies, as well television programs, drew audiences like never before. Early Western film stars like Lash Larue, Tom Mix, and Hoot Gibson were handsome heartthrobs who drove women to movies in record numbers, while beautiful and lusty actresses like Jane Russell and Bette Davis entreated male moviegoers.

Cereal bowl, part of an early children's set featuring Hopalong Cassidy, made by W.S. George Company of Ohio, circa 1950s (see matching plate on page 226). Tooled leather by Silver King Silversmiths.

The original character was created in 1904 and appeared in a series of stories and novels. In 1935 actor William Boyd first starred as the clean cut character in what blossomed into a series of 66 films. He was the only "good guy" to ever wear a black hat. In 1949, NBC made the popular character the subject of the first Western TV series. By 1950, over 100 companies had put Hoppy's likeness on a variety of products, including the first lunchbox and children's Western dinnerware sets. (Courtesy Fred Goodwin, Concept Productions)

"Westerns were to the movies what the sports page is to the daily newspaper: the best part of it."
—**Gene Autry**

The *Gene Autry* Show premiered on CBS in 1950 after establishing huge audiences for a decade as the radio program *Gene Autry's Melody Ranch* on CBS radio. Even his horse Champion had a CBS TV and Radio program, *The Adventures of Champion.* Gene Autry was discovered by the entertainment world in 1934 and had a long and successful career as one of America's favorite singing cowboys. (Courtesy Fred Goodwin, Concept Productions)

Fast action, gushing romance, wild shootouts, and rippling horseflesh made Westerns a visceral experience. Americans loved going to the movies, and in some ways took the experience home with them. The number of cowboy kitsch home accessories seen in the 1950s and '60s has never since been equaled.

One manufacturer in particular, Vernon Kilns of California, put the best of Western film scenes into a home collection called "Bits of the Old West," a set of eight collector plates on which familiar illustrations inspired by classic Westerns were shown. Some of my favorites are the typical stage coach holdup, a train robbery, an ambush, and a stagecoach arrival, all beautifully rendered in full detail.

But by the end of the Western film craze in the late 1960s and early '70s, the stars had moved on, the scripts had changed, and the Western influence in popular culture had begun to wane. The cowboy as a highly visible figure in the entertainment media would not reemerge with such prominence until decades later when country music would transform him into a cross-over rock star, decked in a curled brim hat and tight jeans, minus the horse.

"Art is the only way to run away without leaving home."

—Twyla Thorpe

The statistics tell the story. In 1957–58 for example, there were at least forty to fifty Western television programs. You couldn't live in America and not hear the strains of a harmonica or the clop of horse hooves in your living room. The 1950s institutionalized a national longing for the range that never was—one where horses were always clean, women were beautiful, and outlaws and lawmen looked like movie stars, which they were. Children learned everything from social etiquette to gunplay from watching television. No wonder dinnerware manufacturers sought to tap into the craze. Why wouldn't they?

Behind the ravenous appetite for cinema's escapist stories into the West was, in part, a need to rise above the struggle of everyday life and identify with a respectable hero. A disenchanted America, discouraged first by the Great Depression, and then the challenges of World War II, sought relief from the economic and

wartime worries of the day. Film was everyman's opiate and the Saturday matinee the legitimate house of pleasure.

According to Jeff Hildebrandt, Director of On-Air Promotion at Starz Entertainment, producers of the highly successful Western Channel that replays old Western serials and films, "the Western movie and television shows portrayed a hero with an independent spirit, not tied down to a factory job or struggling on the land. The escape that these stories provided was visual and spiritual—the viewer too could ride into that rugged landscape, suspend their own reality, and feel the tingle of that self-forged independence and freedom."

It's not surprising that the Western has been adopted into other cultures around the world. The need to escape is universal.

Following the end of the Western was a brief interlude where the film world turned to science fiction and the galaxy, a distant cousin of the horse opera or Classic Western. *Star Wars* rocked a nation with a new kind of adventure inspired by our growing space program. As producer George Lucas himself said, "Star Wars was, after all, just another Western."

Even the actors and plot lines of other space films like *Battle Star Galactica* and the series, *Star Trek*, were taken straight out of Western movies, and actors like William Shatner and Leonard Nimoy were, too. By recycling the familiar dramas and faces, Hollywood could extend the power of those old Westerns just a little longer.

Opposite: Each of these plates captures a moment in a classic Western story, from "Bits of the Old West" by Vernon Kilns. Decal transfers, hand painted under glaze. "The Posse"—Sneaking up to the mouth of a canyon; "The Train Robbery"—Pity the poor train travelers trapped within while brigands fired shots on all sides; "The Stage"—The arrival of a stagecoach, safely, was always a miracle; "The Stage Holdup"—sometimes they just didn't make it.

Left: *Maverick*, 1957–1962, a series that actually spoofed Westerns. (Courtesy Bob Anderson, *Trail Dust* magazine)
Above: *Have Gun Will Travel*, 1957–1963, Richard Boone as a gun for hire, known as Paladin. (Courtesy Bob Anderson, *Trail Dust* magazine)
Below: *Hondo*, 1953, John Wayne as Hondo Lane, Ward Bond as Buffalo, Tom Irish as Lt. McKay, and James Arness as Lennie. Arness appeared in this Western feature two years before the *Gunsmoke* series. (Courtesy Bob Anderson, *Trail Dust* magazine)

For those that missed the era, be aware that in addition to the classic "horse opera" (Hollywood's nickname for a formula Western) there were "Samurai" Westerns, "Spaghetti" Westerns (made in Italy), Vampire Westerns, Science Fiction Westerns, Musical Westerns, Cavalry Westerns, Noir Westerns, Psychological Westerns, and Traditional Westerns, to name a few.

Keep in mind that in the decade of the 1940s, a mere 48 Western films made it to the big screen. But between 1950 and 1954, that number jumped to 375 individual titles; from 1955 to 1959, 245 films, and through the mid-1960s, 222 films. The 1970s saw a drop to a total of 88 films, and at least one-third of those were produced in Europe or Japan. The 1980s saw 60 films, and the 1990s, a total of 71 Westerns in all their varieties.

Top: No one loved Westerns more than the Japanese back in the Golden Era of Hollywood Westerns. They had their own brand of them, modeled after Hollywood B movies (Samurai Westerns). Best guess puts this gift plate around 1959–1964. The back simply says "Japan," and it has a nicely anchored hanger.
Left: *Shane*, 1953. Alan Ladd (Shane) shows his fast gun skills to young Brandon de Wilde (Joey Starrett) in this landmark adult Western that helped change the face of Westerns in general. (Courtesy Bob Anderson, *Trail Dust* magazine)

CHAPTER 6

Wearing the Brand

Dinnerware as an Advertising or Promotional Medium

Not surprisingly, the dinner plate eventually became a vehicle for mass-market promotion of Western film actors, just one more piece of Americana that has filled our museums, flea markets, and curio shops.

According to Cheryl Rogers Barnette, a daughter of Roy Rogers and Dale Evans, there were at one time no less than four hundred various products bearing the likeness or name of her father, that beloved cowboy hero whose image made the transition from film and television to things like cereal boxes, home accessories, pajamas, lunch boxes, lampshades, clothing, mini-guitars, games, toys, bedspreads, glasses, and dinnerware. The Roy Rogers Museum, once located in southern California and later in Branson, Missouri, before closing in 2009, actually licensed a manufacturer in the Los Angeles area, Stillmeadow Pottery, to

Classic white with raised rim and gold rope trim. Universal Pottery, founded in Cambridge, Ohio, in 1934, ended its dinnerware production in 1960, and folded in 1976. Also known as Universal Promotions, Inc.

produce an entire set of dinnerware for sale through the museum gift shop, emblazoned with Roy's likeness.

Then and now, Roy stood for American honesty and goodness, without exception. Reinforcement of that message came in many forms.

Promo shots like this were collected by all of Roy's fans and are still circulating today. I heard that Trigger loved to rear on command. (Courtesy Fred Goodwin, Concept Productions)

Back stamp reads: Series: "Slice of Life," Manufacturer 222 Fifth, PTS America." Just one design in a series of American heroes or landmarks on stoneware. Explanation on back states: "Cowboy, illustration by Kent Barton. Nothing conjures up the image of the Old West like the cowboy. This hard working hired hand tended his cattle by day and lulled them to sleep at night with a campfire song. Though he ruled the West a short time, the cowboy continues to influence our culture whether in music, movies, or the clothes we wear. Guess there's a little cowpoke in us all."

Roy Rogers Code of the West "Rider's Rules"

1. Be neat and clean.
2. Be courteous and polite.
3. Always obey your parents.
4. Protect the weak and help them.
5. Be brave but never take chances.
6. Study hard and learn all you can.
7. Be kind to animals and care for them.
8. Eat all your food and never waste any.
9. Love God and go to Sunday School regularly.
10. Always respect our flag and our country.

CHAPTER 7

Dude Ranches

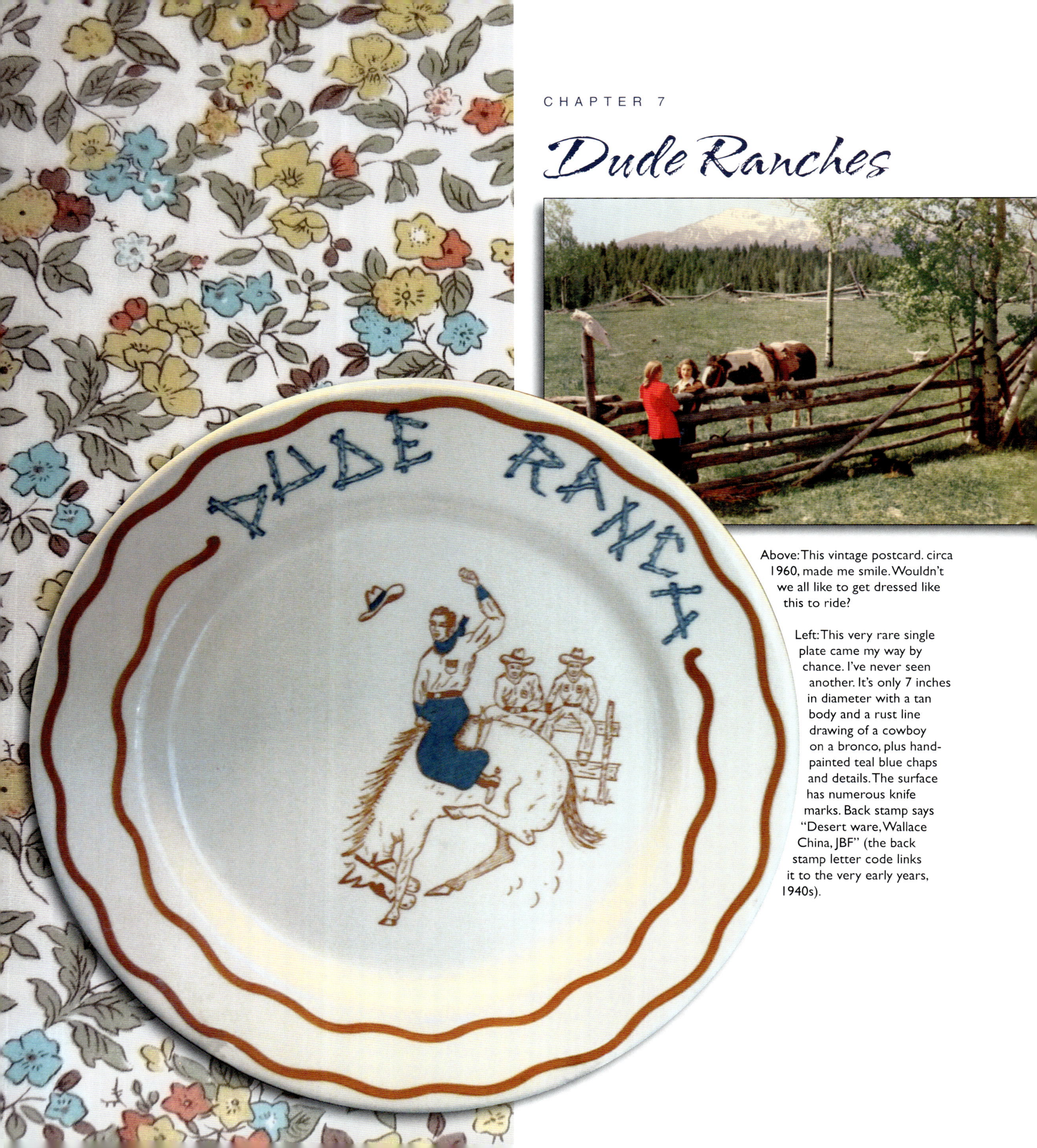

Above: This vintage postcard. circa 1960, made me smile. Wouldn't we all like to get dressed like this to ride?

Left: This very rare single plate came my way by chance. I've never seen another. It's only 7 inches in diameter with a tan body and a rust line drawing of a cowboy on a bronco, plus hand-painted teal blue chaps and details. The surface has numerous knife marks. Back stamp says "Desert ware, Wallace China, JBF" (the back stamp letter code links it to the very early years, 1940s).

In a 1992 article entitled "Dude Dishes" in *Yippee Yi Yea* magazine, writer Julie Semrau stated, "Most novice collectors assume that cowboy china was made exclusively as place settings promoting movie cowboys such as Gene Autry and Hopalong Cassidy, but whole sets of dishes were produced from the 1930s into the 1970s for use by Western dude ranches and for everyday use by families."

Exposure to dude ranches created a demand for tableware that evoked an Old West decorating theme. Customers wanted to bring that feeling home and keep those memories on the table. For many families, dude ranches were, and still are, the ultimate Western vacation. Where else can you saddle up and ride a horse into the wilderness, take part in a round-up and branding, or sit around a campfire enjoying real Western music?

In addition to horses or ranch activities, most ranches have a lake or stream for fly fishing and plenty of opportunities to simply take it easy. There's something special about watching a colorful Western sunset. These days, you're likely to find amenities for soothing body and soul as well, such as hot tubs and spa facilities. On all guest ranches, you can expect to find good times, great food, and in some cases—Western dinnerware.

For the most part, today's dude ranch owners, like restaurateurs, invest in quality restaurant ware that's easy to replace. But many are committed to serving up their meals on Western-themed china, too, going the extra mile to give the ranch guests as much ambiance as he or she can get. Sitting down to a bountiful table decked

Who could possibly resist a spread like this one? Food on a ranch this good deserves a super presentation and it's obvious that the tableware "Westward Ho" by True West does the trick. (Courtesy Home Ranch, Clark, Colorado)

with scenes of cowboy life or a fancy brand on your plate is about as good as it gets.

The history of the dude ranch industry can be traced back to the legendary Eatons' Ranch in Sheridan, Wyoming. Their story begins in 1879, when brothers Howard, Willis, and Alden Eaton established their horse and cattle ranch near Medora, North Dakota. Their friends from the East began to visit them almost immediately. Some of these early guests stayed for months at a time. Finally, one of the guests recognized the expense these extended visits entailed and prevailed upon the Eatons to charge for room and board, so "folks can stay as long as they like." Thus, the dude ranch business was born and an industry started.

Top: This sepia photo shows the Eatons' Ranch in Wolf, Wyoming, as it once was in the late 1800s, a piece of Wyoming history. (Courtesy Paul Harbaugh collection, Denver, CO, with permission of Eatons' Ranch)
Above: The Eatons' Ranch logo appears on all merchandise and tableware. The simple pictograph of a horse is clean and distinctive. (Courtesy Eatons' Ranch)

In 1904, to provide a more suitable and varied riding terrain for their ever-growing number of guests, the Eatons "pulled up stakes" in North Dakota and moved to the present ranch location on Wolf Creek near Sheridan, Wyoming. The Eatons' Ranch has always been in the hands of the Eaton family and is now operated by the third, fourth, and fifth generations of Eatons. So important is the brand of the ranch that it appears on all their stock animals, publicity, and dinnerware. And yes, they have their very own china service, unique to the property.

According to Colleen Hudson, director of the Dude Ranchers' Association headquartered in Cody, Wyoming, "the Western dude ranch could first be considered a vacation destination after visitors became paying guests shortly before the twentieth century. It wasn't until after World War I that visitors came and paid for the experience in much greater numbers. The spike in popularity at this time is often attributed to Henry Ford and the invention of the autombile, as well as the popularity of a new movie genre depicting the thrills and romance of the Old West. Folks from the East came in waves, escaping the heat and crowds of modern city life. Word spread about the special qualities of the dude ranch vacation and it became a national passion."

No matter what they're serving, it looks enticing on True West dinnerware. (Courtesy Home Ranch)

Home Ranch

A ranch that does use commerical Western tableware is the Home Ranch in Clark, Colorado, a year-round resort in Routt County near Steamboat Springs. Complete with spa service, a riding program, adult-only weeks, and so much more, the resort is a member of the prestigious Relais et Chateaux family of Preferred Lodges, a French rating system for exclusive resorts with a major emphasis on food. They look for the unique, not the predictable, and accept only the finest properties.

Chef Clyde Nelson, on board since 1989, learned the *art de cuisine* under Master Chef Anton Flory and went on to improvise, combining the best of classic French cooking with cowboy rustic. He's earned an international reputation for making the dude ranch dining experience exceptional. Nelson says he likes to alternate between casual dining and white tablecloths in the evenings. But more importantly, breakfast and lunch are presented Old West style with buffet items, as well as á la carte dishes, handsomely served on True West Home "Westward Ho" china. Both "Rodeo" and "Boots & Saddle" patterns are used.

"Our guests love the Western china. It's worth the extra investment that it costs to keep and maintain this service. Few who come to the dude ranch have ever seen Western china before. The average fifty-something client finds it charming and evocative of everything they think the West should be. Not only are the cabins here nestled in natural areas, our riding program is one of the top in the industry, but even the food and its presentation has the power to carry our guests into a different dimension. Presentation is everything."

—Chef Nelson

Is it just me or is this the most scrumptious finish to a cowboy lunch ever? (Courtesy Home Ranch)

The kitchen at the Home Ranch tries to maintain a balance, staying grounded but also upscale and sophisticated. They've succeeded. As a committed member of the Dude Ranch Association, President and Manager Johnny Fisher has always emphasized service, and Chef Nelson's decision to stock the pantry with Western-themed china is just one example.

"We have a captive audience for seven days," said Nelson, "so we can treat them to a wide variety of dining experiences, like chuck wagon suppers cooked and enjoyed outdoors, cowboy style, or sit-down service in the dining room. The dishes we use just help set the mood."

Ranch at Rock Creek

Yet one more ranch operation that believes in the "extra mile" is set in the wilds of Montana, near Missoula. The Ranch at Rock Creek, a classic example of rustic and civilized, offers true comfort and great furnishings within, and rugged beauty without. The ranch is also a customer of True West dinnerware, but is in the process of designing their own branded tableware, as well.

Proprietor James Manley, who bought the ranch in 2007, explains that the existing outfit was known as the Rocking K Ranch before then, and the Strand Ranch before that. Manley hails from New Jersey and was obsessed with cowboys as a young boy growing up in the '50s. He watched all the Western films he could and dreamed of owning his own "Ponderosa," a ranch where he could ride horses and run cattle.

After a successful career in the investment business, he started looking for the perfect property. It took him twenty years, but eventually he found the Rocking K. It

Custom china sets a great table. (Courtesy Ranch at Rock Creek)

The main ranch house is warm and inviting, especially by night. (Courtesy Ranch at Rock Creek).

fulfilled his criteria, some of which included being located in a valley between 5,000 and 6,000 feet in elevation, rich with water and surrounded by beautiful scenery. In addition, it couldn't have rattlesnakes! Worth the wait, he found his Ponderosa and undertook a complete renovation. The Ranch at Rock Creek, newly opened in late 2009, is a dude ranch with everything a dude could ask for, including Western dinnerware.

The True West "Rodeo" pattern looks great outdoors. (Courtesy Ranch at Rock Creek)

The Dude Ranchers' Association (DRA) was formed in 1926 to serve the needs of those committed to running this kind of vacation operation. The DRA is a valuable resource for anyone planning a dude ranch vacation.

Western riding and related activities are the chief focus of the authentic dude ranch vacation. But many modern ranches also come with swimming pools, golf course access, mountain bike trails, archery and skeet-shooting ranges, trout streams and ponds, and whitewater rafting.

Through the years, ranchers have adapted to the needs and desires of guests. Today, guests can enjoy full-service pampering, world-class shopping, and gourmet food and wine. Some travelers choose a "working ranch" experience, spending long days in the saddle moving cattle. Offering a range of activities and often special programs for kids as well, Western ranches are often selected as sites for multi-generation family reunions. Having weathered the test of time, adapting to society as needed, the traditional Western dude ranch vacation lives on.

CHAPTER 8

Restaurant Ware Then and Now

Custom Branded China

Left: This cartoon steer, Mr. Moo, was the logo most familiar to patrons of Western Sizzlin' Steak House back when it first started. It appeared on dishware, placemats, signage, and matches. Today the company is all grown up.

Below: These days, Mr. Moo has turned into a skateboarding dude, seen on placemats for kids. (Courtesy Western Sizzlin')

Western imagery has been used to sell everything from hot dogs to cigarettes to four-wheel drives, and it has prevailed as an effective means to woo the consumer for over a century. Restaurant chains that launched back in the 1960s and '70s were no exception, especially steakhouses. Some used Western décor and a Western logo even if the cuisine wasn't really cowboy—and even if they weren't located in the West—but the formula worked, then as now.

Some of these early Western restaurant brands are still familiar names today, with loyal customers that have dined with them for decades, such as Ponderosa Steakhouse, Bonanza Steakhouse, Western Sizzlin' (ironically from the Deep South), Black Angus Steakhouse, and Trail Dust Steak House, to name a few.

According to Sheryl Randolph, Vice President of Marketing at Ponderosa and Bonanza Restaurants, "We're proud of our Western steakhouse heritage, and although we offer an expansive variety of foods on our buffet, steaks are a critical piece of our business. Both Ponderosa and Bonanza brands have evolved throughout the decades, sometimes forgetting our Western heritage, but we have recently made a deliberate effort to return to our heritage and strengths in serving affordable steaks in a family-friendly, Western environment. We are looking at each touch point for the consumer throughout the dining experience, so that we recreate a uniquely warm Western hospitable experience that will leave our guests craving more. We know that consumers 'eat with their eyes,' so plateware is one of the many details that we will leverage to reignite our Western heritage, as it can elevate the experience and set the tone for an emotional connection to our steakhouses."

Possibly a salad plate, kept chilled in the buffet stack, or a bread and butter plate, this milk glass type plate and its matching cup (not shown) were part of Ponderosa tableware according to Pyrex historians.

A newer generation of steakhouses emerged in the 1980s, such as Longhorn Steakhouse, Lone Star Restaurants, and Texas Roadhouse, to name a few, and they grew in popularity, as consumers seemed to still have a love of great steaks in a casual and somewhat authentic Western environment. Today, the urban landscape is dotted with these and still more, such as Outback Steakhouse (off the Australian frontier), and Ted's Montana Grill (a combination of upscale Western with a "green" emphasis). These newer Western eateries' menus still revolve mostly around beef, but the message and the

Shuller's Wig Wam must have been everybody's favorite lunch and dinner spot in College Hill, Ohio.(Photos by Lindsay Allen)

market focus have changed. For many, the target is less family-oriented and more upscale, with a décor that's both rugged and sophisticated. Simply stated, they have embraced the feel of the West, but wrapped in a notably modern twist.

Here's a look back in time to some of the earlier Western-inspired tableware used by restaurants across the country.

The simplest sandwich looks wonderful on a Shuller's plate.

Shuller's Wig Wam

The WigWam opened back in 1922 and was originally owned by Max and Anna Shuller, Russian immigrants who brought their ethnic cuisine with them. The service began as a small hamburger stand with seating for six and grew rapidly until the menu was loaded with hearty European fare. In 1934, they added a beer garden with a glass enclosure, and then in the 1940s for some unexplained reason built a giant tepee-shaped addition that gave the location a highly noticeable appearance. Hence, the "WigWam" name.

By 1954, the tepee was torn down and replaced with a standard building featuring two dining rooms and twelve party rooms. But the name "Shuller's WigWam" stayed, along with the distinctive china made by Bailey Walker China (Toltecware) with the Indians on horseback. The restaurant became part of the town's history as a favored site for family gatherings, wedding receptions, and other occasions. A local radio personality, Jean Shepard, broadcast radio shows from the restaurant for many years. The operation ceased to exist in 2000.

Rod's Steak House, Williams, Arizona

Rod's Steak House was established in 1946, during the heyday of historic Route 66. Located sixty miles south of the Grand Canyon, Rod's is a world-famous restaurant visited by people from around the world. The much sought-after menu, die-cut in the shape of a steer, proudly boasts all-American food.

The current owners, the third since its inception, Lawrence and Stella Sanchez, proudly keep the old traditions alive. Lawrence has been proprietor of the establishment for twenty-five years. Prior to that, he had been manager and head chef for an additional eleven years. Over that time, he's seen thousands of customers, many Americans reliving a nostalgic trip into the past, along with brand new patrons, following the beloved highway of the 1950s across the West on the famed Route 66.

Above: This vintage menu dates from the 1940s or '50s. The same design can be found in use today. Right: The china service shown here and produced by Syracuse China portrayed the classic Rod's Steakhouse logo. This dinnerware is still in use.

Rod's branded china plates and accessories are among the many pieces of memorabilia that seem to be traded among collectors. "The china was originally made by the Wallace China company back in the 1940s and '50s," said Sanchez. "Up until recently, the supplier was Syracuse China. All this time, we've continued using our distinctive logo of the Hereford steer whose image defines our menu. We're still serving honest American food and are open for lunch and dinner seven days a week."

Western Sizzlin'

According to Western Sizzlin's company history, "In 1962 in Augusta, Georgia, company founder Nick Pascarella discovered a unique way of grilling steaks. If searing the bottom of the steak made it juicy, he reasoned that adding flames to the top would make them twice as good. He was absolutely right and the world famous FlameKist® steak was born. This unique process locks in the flavor as the steak is seared to a savory perfection.

Nick's concept was just too good to keep to himself. In 1966, he responded to requests and began selling franchises nationally. The company has persisted to this day, evolving with the times and still offering great food. In addition to steaks, other entrees include chicken and seafood, plus country vegetables and fresh baked breads and desserts. Although the amusing cartoonish cow that appeared on plates and placemats, Mr. Moo, has been dropped, many can remember when heading to Western Sizzlin' for flavorful beef brought out a little cowboy in us all.

Here's a restaurant company that knows how to make a meal appear as tempting as possible. Is it the steak, or the effect of the modern-day steak platter, an obvious replica of a cast iron griddle. (Courtesy Western Sizzlin')

CHAPTER 9

The Revival

Everyone Loves a Comeback

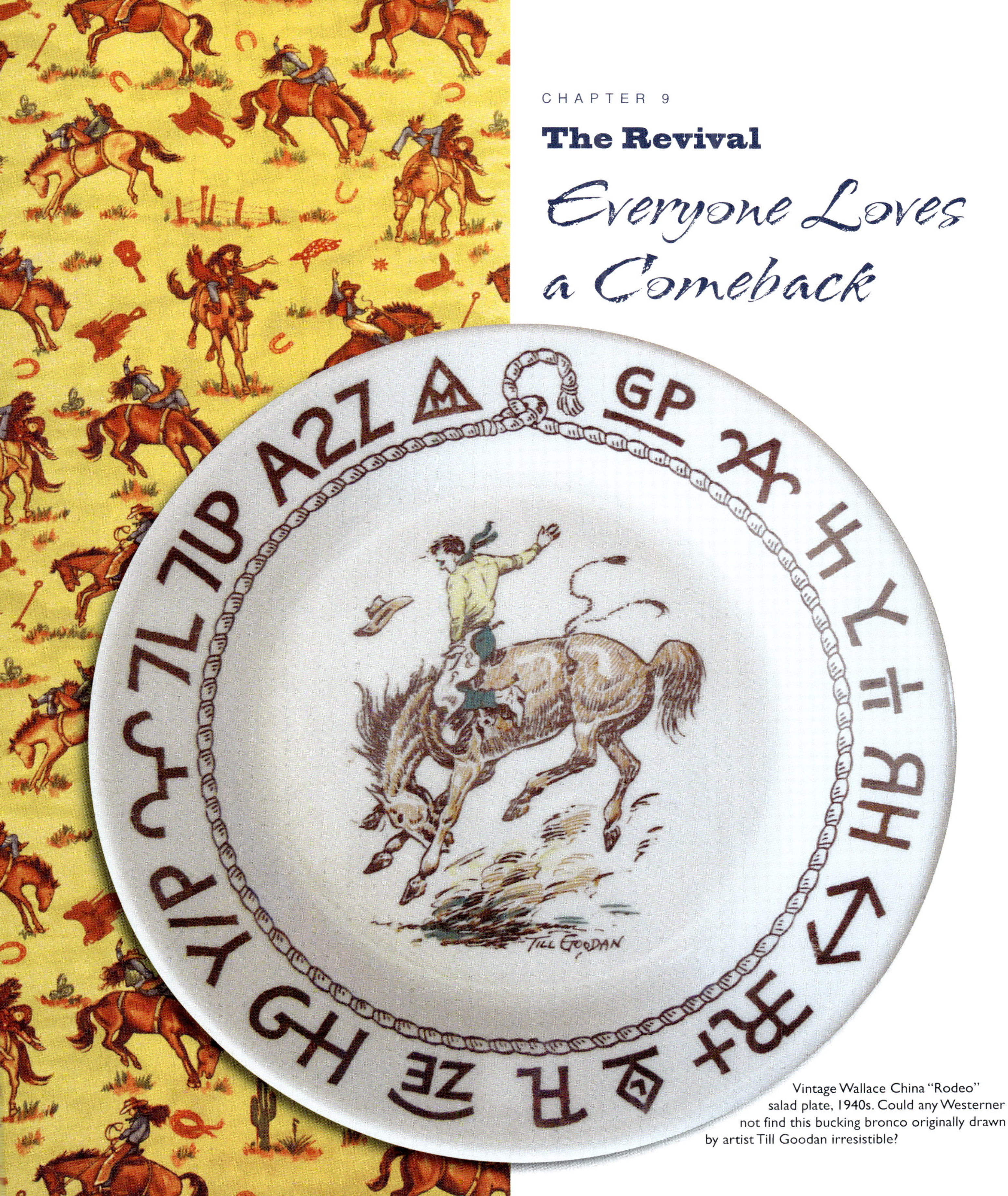

Vintage Wallace China "Rodeo" salad plate, 1940s. Could any Westerner not find this bucking bronco originally drawn by artist Till Goodan irresistible?

Stillmeadow Pottery porcelain—decal of team ropers doing what cowboys do best.

After the Western craze peaked in the late 1960s and '70s, the 1980s and '90s were quieter years. Mainstream stores carried little that resembled the earlier mania. But like an undercurrent, the spirit of the West was just below the surface.

In the case of Western dinnerware, a few singular producers made patterns for the homeowner. Most of the bigger national potteries focused on hotel and restaurant supply to survive the tsunami of Asian imports in ceramics, or they didn't survive at all.

On the West Coast during the quiet years, Stillmeadow Pottery continued to manufacture tableware and sell directly, making custom ware for ranches, individuals, and businesses. Back East, another small independent manufacturer named Pipestone made a spectacular splash in the 1980s with work by Texas artist Buckeye Blake, a remarkable collection that came and went.

But as is often the case, when the time is ripe, new ideas have a way of occurring simultaneously. Around the year 2000, two firms, Montana Silversmiths (Lifestyles) and Cowboy Living, both launched new collections geared toward the individual consumer. They were after the mass market nationwide. The following year also marked the official reorganization of True West Home, the Texas reincarnation of the vintage firm Wallace China.

Something told these ambitious entrepreneurs that it was time for the cowboy to return. As profiles in subsequent chapters will illustrate, these three dinnerware

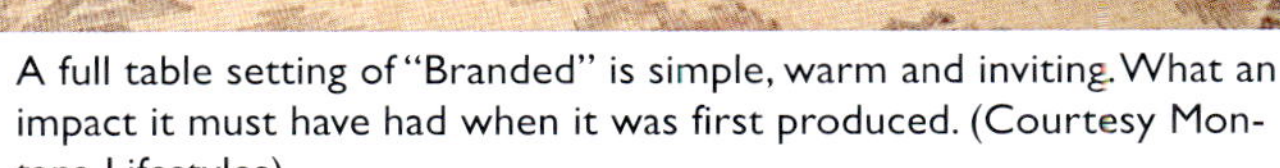

A full table setting of "Branded" is simple, warm and inviting. What an impact it must have had when it was first produced. (Courtesy Montana Lifestyles)

producers came out strong. From the first reception, their products have merely whetted the public's appetite for more.

According to Pat Turner at True West Home, the collector's market for Western china needed to be served. "There was a big demand for vintage Wallace china, especially a pattern group known as "Westward Ho," a genre favorite. Little of the actual vintage ware was in circulation anymore, yet interest was high. It was an opportunity whose time had come" (see page 126).

The new millennium had much to offer with three viable Western companies to choose from, each creating designs independently and targeting a hungry audience. Like the end of a summer drought, Western dinnerware was back.

The Love Affair Continues

So what graces the surfaces of Western dinnerware pieces today? Not the hardy drover of old, it appears. At the moment, the hottest recognizable cowboy in popular culture seems to be the Marlboro Man, a persona with no name but a clearly defined image that stands for self-styled individualism and Western independence. Billboards and magazine ads have made sure we know the stance, the profile, and the shadowed face of the one man who continues to represent the West. Always the consummate cowboy, he's become the James Bond of the frontier, fulfilling a male fantasy. No rowdy start-up, this cowboy has seen some miles and projects his success (and the brand's) with self-confidence and authority.

Richard Aquila, in *Wanted Dead or Alive: The American West in Popular Culture,* sums it up nicely.

"Philip Morris began using this figure [a cowboy] exclusively in 1964. Twelve years later, Marlboro was the best selling cigarette in the United States and the world. These ads have epitomized the West as a place. The Marlboro Man works in Marlboro Country, a land of majestic mountains and wild, wide spaces. How he looks and what he does tell of life that has him supremely independent, utterly at ease in Eden, self-contained, as tough as his saddle. Anyone responding to these ads is buying an uncompromised dream of westering."

Second to this Western demi-God, it seems that today we really have no single national cowboy hero. The vote (for those in the know) might divide between famous pro-rodeo stars like Ty Murray (retired) or Trevor Brazile, current world champion PRCA rodeo cowboy, or crooners like the authentic Westerner, George Strait, or the late Chris LeDoux, a real cowboy who combined rodeo with music to great success.

Whoever it might be, it appears that the celluloid version of the cowboy will never again see the likes of John Wayne, a man who as far back as the 1930s was a national hero who rode into America's heart in dozens of films that proved his immense staying power and appeal. Instead, we waiver between reruns of Clint Eastwood in his prime, and great Western movies with Robert Duvall, Tom Selleck, and Sam Elliott, among others. All respectable in their cowboy roles, it's doubtful any one of them will become as enduring as the Duke.

Like the Phillip Morris company, Western dinnerware manufacturers have turned to the powerful silhouette of the universal cowboy instead. Various portrayals

The Searchers, 1956, John Wayne as Ethan Edwards and his son Patrick Wayne as Lt. Greenhill, in the John Ford classic about John Wayne's driven character who brings a young girl back from her Indian captors. To this day, "The Duke" is the one Hollywood actor who needs no introduction—he defined the American Western movie with his bigger than life persona and left a legacy that hasn't dimmed. (Courtesy Bob Anderson, *Trail Dust* magazine)

A cowboy heads after his catch in a cloud of dust with rope poised. A masterful shot by photographer David Stoecklein, whose black and white and full color images of the cowboy are known around the world. (Courtesy David Stoecklein)

Left: "Western Flains" by Clay Art in San Francisco. Artwork portrays the universal horseman against a boldly lit airbrushed sky. Hand air brushed salad plate with twisted rope border (one of a three piece set).
Right: "Top Hand" photo taken at the TS Ranch, Nevada, by internationally recognized American photographer Acam Jahiel, who lives and works in the American West. His poetic and dynamic images have been exhibited and published world wide. His photographs are in the collections of the Nevada Art Museum in Reno, the Art Institute of Chicago, the Museum of Fine Arts in Boston, as well as private and corporate collections. (Copyright 1995 by Adam Jahiel)

show him in action—in the arena, roping a steer, or riding into the sunset.

Some dinnerware producers have eliminated the cowboy altogether and replaced him with colors, textures, and patterns. Who doesn't recognize the bold flash of black and white cowhide, the casual texture and familiar color of faded blue denim, or the sensual surface of tooled leather?

Time has only to pass for us to see what's in store tomorrow, for the cowboy will always be a part of America—a symbol of our Western spirit. And the dinner table will always be the gathering place for friends and family, not only to celebrate life's special moments, but also to define who we are and how we want to be known.

CHAPTER 10

Children's Western Dinnerware

The elements of the old West seem to have been made for children's play. Back in the 1940s and '50s, American children were naturally drawn to the afternoon Western serials and the excitement of cowboy versus Indian, or of a posse in pursuit of an armed bandit.

Playing at cowboys felt empowering—for little boys *and* girls. Television and Western movies introduced the younger set to all kinds of notions about life, conflicts, and solutions to problems. The Western scene in which cowboys fought Indians was for many the only concept they had of Native Americans, good or bad. In many scenes where pioneers gathered in covered wagons, it seemed like hostile Indian forces were always just beyond the ridge. (Thank goodness for the Lone Ranger, whose personal sidekick Tonto was both an Indian and a loyal friend.)

With war whoops and hollers, children's playtime often consisted of some version of braves on the warpath or a posse on the run. Dinnerware manufacturers were quick to see the marketing possibilities.

Back then, as now, children's dinnerware was a specialty—gift-packed with multiple pieces, sometimes

Dinner plate from "Montana Baby," the centerpiece of a five-piece Melamine child's set by Montana Lifestyles. The simple design speaks to the child in all of us—warm and colorful.

Hopalong Cassidy, two of three pieces made by the W.S. George Company of Ohio, circa 1950s–'60s. These two are in pristine condition; matching plate shown on p. 123.

Milk glassware made by the popular Hazel Atlas Company was a viable alternative to china. It wore well, was dishwasher safe, and attractive. This vintage child's set, 1950s, is one of my favorites.

Sturdy Hazel Atlas glass mugs were sized for little fingers. My favorite shows Tex the Marshall marching his outlaw captive to jail!

with matching plastic ware, a spoon, and a fork. Items were presented in attractive sets, usually including a plate, a cereal bowl, and a cup or mug. The subjects portrayed during the golden age of Western dinnerware reflected cowboy heroes of the day, as well as scenes of cowboy life—cookouts, bronc busters, and cowboys and Indians.

But a growing concern for political correctness and respect for various ethnicities cancelled out most images of Indians by the 1960s.

Los Angeles manufacturer Peco Ware has been making their children's set for over twenty-five years, showing a charming mounted cowboy on his horse. On close examination, there's a teepee in the background, too, but no visible Indians.

Earlier, in the '50s, the Hazel Atlas Company made a wonderful children's set in white milk

For the littlest cowboy or cowgirl, Peco Ware of California has created a classic here. I love the fact that a toddler can drop these dishes on the floor and they won't break. The details are charming and the set comes beautifully packaged in a decorative box.

glass, one with cowboys and Indians, and yet another with a Texas marshal taking his captive to jail! Even Walt Disney Productions made a plastic set with cowboy Mickey waving his hat while astride his rearing horse.

Wallace China and artist Till Goodan created an endearing set known as "Little Buckaroo." To quote collector Janet Hix of Texas, "What child wouldn't want to finish his cereal to see the little cowpoke waving at him from the bottom?"

Even after the industry became monopolized by Japanese imports in the 1960s and '70s, a series of thematic Western children's cups continued to be designed with a new, whimsical sensibility. In their own way, they

Above: Bunnykins' children's set by Royal Doulton, circa 1972. A child's cup with all the terror of the struggles between the Plains Indians and the pioneers. No nursery rhymes here, just a decoration trying to keep in step with the times. Left: Plastic was all the rage in the 1960s and this Disney cup was probably part of a whole set. Who knew Mickey Mouse had a secret life as a cowboy?

are full of charm. In a modern world of global threats, terrorism, and an arsenal of children's toys shaped like robotic transformers and aliens, it doesn't seem likely that today's children will play at cowboys any more. But one can only hope.

Top: From the private collection of Janet Hix, "Little Buckaroo," original vintage children's set made by Wallace China circa 1950. All the accessories are vintage, too. Note the exceptional leather placemat.
Left: Wallace back stamp of "Little Buckaroo ware." (All courtesy Janet Hix)

This children's cup seems to suggest a cup of hot chocolate and a bedtime story. It evokes the sentiment and whimsy that went into designing Western dinnerware for children. Made in Japan, circa 1950s.

This incredible find, produced in the 1950s by Taylor Smith and Taylor (1899–1982, in Chester, West Virginia, purchased by Anchor Hocking in 1973) is a rare vestige of the famed *Howdy Doody Show*. This iconic children's program aired on NBC from 1947 to 1960. Its various characters made the West a friendly place, including clown Clarabell, Chief Thunderthud, Princess Summerfall Winterspring and Buffalo Bob himself, Bob Smith. Howdy, the freckled puppet with the red bandana, was derived from the greeting, "Howdy Do!"

CHAPTER 11

Paper and Plastic

Eating outdoors means no fuss, so plastic is always acceptable. Picnics come to life with a cowboy theme. Here, Melamine plates by ModaHome (right) and Triple Creek (left) do the job.

Disposable paper and plastic ware are so common in our society that we take them entirely for granted. Sturdier ware is made of plastic, in a variety of colors. But if you're looking for something more, with a recognizable theme, especially Western, the choices are many at crafts stores, paper emporiums, and party shops. In addition, housewares sections of many department and specialty stores carry Western-themed goods made of Melamine.

Durability and practicality are just two of the reasons you might want your dinnerware to be the unbreakable kind. Tailgating, cooking out, and picnicking are just a few occasions where ceramics won't work. Manufacturers like Moda International and Triple Creek are just two suppliers that offer grand choices in durable Melamine, with designs that will never go out of style.

Paper manufacturers offer a wide range of choices you can use, enjoy, and toss when you're done. Look for manufacturer names like Caspari, ("Denim" by Chuck Fischer), Amscan's "Bandana Ranch," Creative Converting's "Out West," and Bag of Chips Productions' "Cowboy."

"Giddy Up" plastic ware by Triple Creek is a useful and fun accessory to any outdoor event, rodeo, or family reunion. A full set makes a party. (Courtesy Triple Creek)

Top: A Western themed-birthday party for children has always been one of my favorites. All that's missing here is a cowboy magician and a trick pony. (Note: my two dogs ate all the ice cream out of an open half-gallon container while we were shooting this shot!) (Photo by Lindsay Allen)
Above: Unopened package of paperware dinner plates featuring the Pioneer West, circa 1940s or '50s. Price for the package, $.49. Even back then, America had Western disposable ware.

CHAPTER 12

Motifs The Stories that Shape Us

Little is known about who made this plate since it isn't marked, but it is consistent with products produced by the Fred Roberts Company. It appears to have been inspired by Wallace's "Westward Ho" because of the brands, so a good estimate is 1940s-50s. No back stamp. Made in Japan. See matching cup on page 164.

What makes Western-themed dinnerware so fascinating to me is the variety of subjects and illustrations used by the china companies who turned to the West for inspiration. But they weren't the only ones—magazine illustration and advertising did, too.

In *Wanted Dead or Alive: The American West in Popular Culture*, author Richard Aquila again says it best:

"Advertisers have drawn heavily and often on the Western myth. If no medium has been in closer communion with the mass mind than advertising, no popular tradition is more deeply entrenched in American culture than the Western . . .

"Modern advertising and the West have had a common interactive history. By the 1920s, manufacturers were making their products more alluring by manipulating the consumers' aspirations and anxieties. As executives reached out to a mass market, it became part of their job to gauge the current American mood and then appeal to American customers through their deeply rooted values. One of the best expressions of those values, the Western, made its appearance during those same years. The generation that saw advertising transformed also read from the first Western novels, watched the flourish and decline of Wild West shows, and saw the earliest Western films and movie stars. ... From then until now, advertising and the Western myth have been an enduring combination."

Products created for mass consumption generally followed trends that made the most amount of money. What's hot in the news can make itself felt on the fashion runway, on the toy shelf, or in the living and dining room. The West was no exception.

Over the decades, recurring images of cowboys, horses, boots, hats, ropes, guns, and saddles, as well as bucking broncos, Longhorn steers, and even the landscape itself, have been put on home furnishings, textiles, and dinnerware. These were not random decisions. The West sells.

Vintage advertisement, dated 1956, for Swift Meats, Greeley, Colorado (currently known as JBB USA LLC). The smiling little cowboy is a perfect example of how the West and food marketing came together. Way back then, every kid wanted to be a cowboy.

More recently, the all-American cowgirl has emerged as a new subject, rightfully taking her place.

Some dinnerware illustrations are actually signed, acknowledging the contribution of specific talent. Others remain anonymous, the contributor unknown When seen as a collective body of work, as a continuum created over time, dinnerware makes a richly decorative and meaningful display that confirms not only the impact of the West in our everyday life, but our changing perceptions of it. From the literal to the nearly abstract, each rendering or decoration is a visual reminder of a larger story and outlook.

The reader is invited to look for these motifs as expressed by the various manufacturers. Like a musical refrain, they return again and again, reinforcing a symbolic vocabulary that has become part of the visual language of Western culture.

Don't you love the crisp action and design of these contemporary plates? Made for Kohl's Inc. under their in-house home décor brand "Sonoma Lifestyles." Each plate shows a rodeo cowboy in action: a roper, a saddle bronc rider, and bareback bronc rider. Assorted hats, barbed wire, and Longhorns appear in the background and around the rim. Stoneware, with heavy vitreous glaze. Made in China.

Some images, like the cowboy, have evolved based on his changing roles, real and fictionalized. Over time, we've seen him morph from a nomadic ranch hand into an invincible icon who stands for righteousness and vanquishes evil.

Other images, like the pioneer traveling West in a covered wagon, have all but disappeared in today's market. That story now seems obsolete, relegated to pioneer museums and history books. It's hard to imagine that what was once our greatest national challenge, the story of the Western migration, has been eclipsed by more contemporary dramas.

Today's artists and illustrators explore a more relevant West, loaded with a new kind of romance. A quick look at the subject matter of modern day manufacturers reveals more contemporary depictions of round-ups, rodeos, roping, and ranch life.

Some manufacturers have also attempted a bold return to the past with a more vintage look, trying to recapture a time when the West was bound by barbed wire, Longhorns, and man's limitless imagination.

What Makes it Western?

So just what makes it Western? Images of brands, barbed wire, the Texas Lone Star, or a pattern of horseshoes? To some, these motifs speak loud and clear. To others, they might be meaningless. It's up to you. The answer for me is continually redefined the longer I collect. In this book, I've included at least one plate that might never be found in another's collection, but to my eye was a sure fit.

Consider the "Roselyn Castle Grill" plate, a stagecoach scene made by Shenango China, circa 1954 (and earlier). If you think it was included here because of the stagecoach, take another look. The vehicle seems to predate the heavier frontier stage like a Wells Fargo or McClellan coach. It almost looks Colonial, as does the residence it passes by, a place named the Red Lion Inn. Such a place has existed since the late 1700s in Stockbridge, Massachusetts, but after making contact, they have no claim on this production.

Notice the remarkable floral border, one that also shows up in Western fashion and other products around the same time. You've seen it on leather carving, Western shirts in the '40s and '50s, embroidery, boot inlay, and any number of Western accessories.

The floral border was probably inspired from English tableware or any of the many hundreds of floral motifs so popular in American transferware at that time. These patterns were, in turn, probably borrowed from earlier patterns created in China or Japan that the West eventually made its own. The petaled flower, most often a type of rose (a dog rose, or wood rose), is a favored decoration. I may be the only collector to include this plate in a Western collection, but to my eye it's a wonderful fit.

What better place to find roses than on your toes, heels, and twining up your ankles? These boots were designed by and for me and made by Tres Outlaws, El Paso, Texas, in 2005.

Much of the western clothing produced around this time by various Western manufacturers relied heavily on floral themes. Men wore floral prints as well as women, no questions asked. In fact, back then, American fashion included Western wear.

According to Dan DeWeese, a freelance writer and Western fashion resource, as well as one of the authors of

According to some china dealers, the large divided 10-1/4 inch grill plate was made by Shenango China for Red Lion restaurants. Extensive research into a few establishments by this name hasn't unearthed a single claimant. The back of the plate is stamped "Roselyn Castle Grill Plate, Shenango China, Newcastle PA." It was made in both red (pink) and blue.

Above: A current shirt with a vintage design from Rockmount Ranch Wear, based on their own archive of classic Western shirts. Just one of many floral embroidery motifs. (Courtesy Steve Weil, Rockmount Ranch Wear)

Left: Leather notebook cover with silver horse head and wild rose silver belt buckle from the creative hands of Silver King, Chatsworth, California, a family business specializing in traditional silver work and leather carving. Other leather creations include belts, albums, handbags, tack and other goods. The rose is handled especially well by their talented team. (Notebook photo by Silver King.)

Made by Scully, Western Leather, Clothing and Accessories since 1906. Black and white gabardine shirt with wild rose appliqué, embroidery, and pearl snaps, circa 2000.

Western Shirts—A Classic American Fashion (along with Steve Weil of Rockmount Ranch Wear), "The 1940s and '50s became known as the Golden Age of Western Shirts, based not only on the popularity of the new style, but on the sheer artistry and construction that went into many of the 'production' shirts."

Over time, the fancy decoration of these shirts waned, especially the time-consuming embroidery, and the garments evolved instead to a more practical, everyday appearance that relied on sturdy fabric types and surface patterns, especially plaids, stripes, and color-block solids. The needs of the working cowboy were paramount, and the fancy embellished shirt was reserved for special occasions and entertainers.

By the current decade, a tremendous interest in the idea of vintage or revival styles spurred a new inventory of designs reflecting embroidered details, especially those by companies like Rockmount Ranch Wear, Scully, and Panhandle Slim. The difference this time around was that the elaborate embroidery and handwork was all done by machine and made offshore, the only way to afford such luxurious decoration.

But the emphasis here is on recurrence: whether it was florals, brands, or broncos, a variety of visual themes of the West have become the symbols of our Western story and are seen again and again. See how many you can come across. You might be surprised.

I was all of sixteen years old here on my beloved horse Danny, circa 1964. I'm wearing a Miller Stockman Western shirt with pearl snap buttons and snap pockets. It was my very favorite—pale blue with flowers everywhere.

Westward, the Pioneer Motif

"Our West"—A Vast Empire Conquered By the Dreams of Pioneers and Colored by The History of Their Descendants. A remarkable tableau by Vernon Kilns for their popular collector plate series. This is a first edition dated 1942. Backstamp reads: "Horace Greeley said 'Go West, young man and grow up with the country.' While he had vision and could see the possibilities of the great western expanse of natural resources, even he did not visualize the vast empire that would be built in such a short period of time. Where the pioneers but yesterday rested their wagons trains, today, great cities are teeming with life and activity. The settlement and building of the West in such a short space of time is one of the outstanding accomplishments of a group of hardy pioneers who had a great vision." Note the highly detailed scenes: Gold panner, bottom; cowpuncher and logger, left; the Alamo, upper center; tall ships, upper right; wagon train, lower right; steam locomotive center; great city rising, center top.

This Wallace dinner plate from the "Pioneer Trails" series may have one of the best images of the prairie schooner, or covered wagon, ever drawn. Six oxen pull this one over the trail, circa 1950s.

America extended both its boundaries and its larger sense of itself in the land rush that brought settlers across the Great Plains all the way to California and Oregon. According to historian Frederick Jackson Turner, this remarkable event transformed our national character as man reshaped his responses to the new world, one that required fresh thinking and self reliance, not adherence to old ways.

The pioneer was the hero of the mid-1800s, and he came West by the thousands in Conestoga wagons pulled by oxen, at best traveling ten to fifteen miles per day. The grueling task of making one's way across the sun-beaten landscape while fording streams and warding off hostile Indian attacks is almost unthinkable in today's world of tamer risks and challenges. It's hard to imagine that just average families, many with young children, undertook the passage. But the passion was real, and the thirst for a new life could only be quenched by staking a claim on a piece of the new frontier.

"A lot of families headed West with no more than bedding, buckets, bibles, and high hopes. That's a pretty good start."

—Anonymous

Royal China

The Royal China Company of Sebring, Ohio, was an American legend, and is much collected today by Americans whose families used its dishware for generations. Founded in 1934, they had a long and successful run until 1986, a victim of a changing global economy and foreign imports.

During their long history, the company had various owners and investors. Like their many competitors, their production was targeted at the American home market, served by a wide choice of non-vitrified household china items. A vitrified (hard and "glassy") ware was also manufactured for government and restaurant use.

The wonderful Currier and Ives plate shown is a perfect example of what they did best: underglaze printing where a monochromatic image was stamped with roller- applied color, a technique that produced a high number of prints per minute. This pattern was run for many years.

No wonder so many artists chose to capture this unique time in our history. Considering it was one of the first themes to be explored in the arts and the mediums of popular culture in the late 1940s and throughout the '50s, one can only wonder why this emotion-charged subject fell out of fashion, now an almost forgotten part of our past.

Some might find it out of the ordinary to include yet another plate destined for the masses made by Royal China in a book about Western-themed dinnerware. But herein lies the joy of collecting—as I said earlier, you can set your own rules.

To this collector, the blue and white transfer image evoked various illustrators who explored the Western migration. The minute I discovered it, I knew it felt familiar, not just that it was a decal version of the famed Currier and Ives print that I had seen before in my career, but I just knew that I had also seen that image somewhere on canvas.

Blue transfer ware of Currier and Ives print. Back stamp reads "The Rocky Mountains," underglaze print by Royal. The original image was called "The Rocky Mountains: Emigrants Crossing the Plains," after the original painting by Albert Bierstadt, and is shown on the next page courtesy of The Old Print Shop, NYC, New York, originally published by Currier and Ives. Drawn on the stone by Fanny F. Palmer (1812–1876), the hand-colored lithograph dates from 1866.

Depicts covered wagon train crossing a valley. The New York based printmaking firm of Currier & Ives produced some of the most popular American art of the 19th century. Founded by Nathaniel Currier and James Merritt Ives in 1866, they specialized in publishing hand-colored lithographic prints that were sold inexpensively to the growing American middle class and were widely collected.

Indeed, Currier and Ives, master printmakers, based their print on an earlier painting by master painter Alfred Bierstadt (1830–1902), once considered the greatest painter of the American West. No simple observer, Bierstadt's large-scale canvases done in the Hudson River style (wherein man is secondary to the grandeur of the landscape) were fictionalized locales, paintings that immortalized the West as a mythological landscape of towering heights, deep valleys, streaming sunshine, and celestial clouds. Here, the pioneer was a welcome denizen of a brave new world, destined to take his rightful place. That this painting was translated to print and then to a transfer for china tableware is an evolution I think Bierstadt himself would have loved. It seems fitting to think that this image reached the common man through the ultimate domestic type of houseware—pottery.

This stirring painting by Albert Bierstadt (1830–1902) created a scene of pastoral beauty in which the pioneers walk under an ethereal, light-filled sky into a kind of wilderness paradise. The artist actually went on several overland journeys of the Western Expansion, and in 1859 found himself in the Wind River Range in Wyoming, an experience that he compared to visiting the European Alps. (Courtesy National Cowboy and Western Heritage Museum, Oklahoma City, Oklahoma)

"Art is either plagiarism or revolution."

—Paul Gauguin

This plate was in fact part of a series celebrating epic American moments. According to Dave Folckmer, current president of the Royal China Association and author of the only book on Royal China, *Royal China Company, Sebring, Ohio*, the company was in business from 1934 until 1986. The plate shown here was called "Rocky Mountains" and measured about eleven inches wide with tab handles. It was first made in 1951 and continued to be made through 1974. A second version was an eleven-inch round platter without the tab handles but with the same scene, made from 1974 until the end of 1986.

This charming plate was manufactured by the J&G Meakin Company of England, a company founded in 1851 and known for making vast quantities of ironstone ware for domestic and export use. The back stamp of this piece dates from between 1958 and 1961, reflecting the shift to modernist forms in dinnerware (note the rounded square shape). The company was taken over by Wedgwood, went defunct in 2000, and the factory was demolished in 2005.

The Mother's Day Plate "Western Trail" collector's plate measuring 5 inches in diameter, artwork by artist Sven Vestergaard, released by Royal Copenhagen in 1988. The theme isn't the pioneer story as much as it is the relationship between mother and daughter, set in a mythic setting. Nonetheless, of all the scenic choices possible, it's interesting to see a depiction like this so late in the decade. For Europeans, our Western past endures.

Royal did some of their best work in the 1950s and '60s, and the Currier and Ives pattern was so popular that it was sold by most big retailers and by catalog mail order, including Sears, Spiegel, J.C. Penny, and Montgomery Ward, just to name a few. It was also used as a premium by most grocery stores, including A&P, Safeway, and Acme, and often given away in boxes of soap and cereal, as well as by banks and gas stations. The Currier and Ives dinnerware was manufactured in six colors—blue, pink, green, black, brown, and multi-colored.

Perhaps you have your own plate by Royal China that tells this Western story: cherish it.

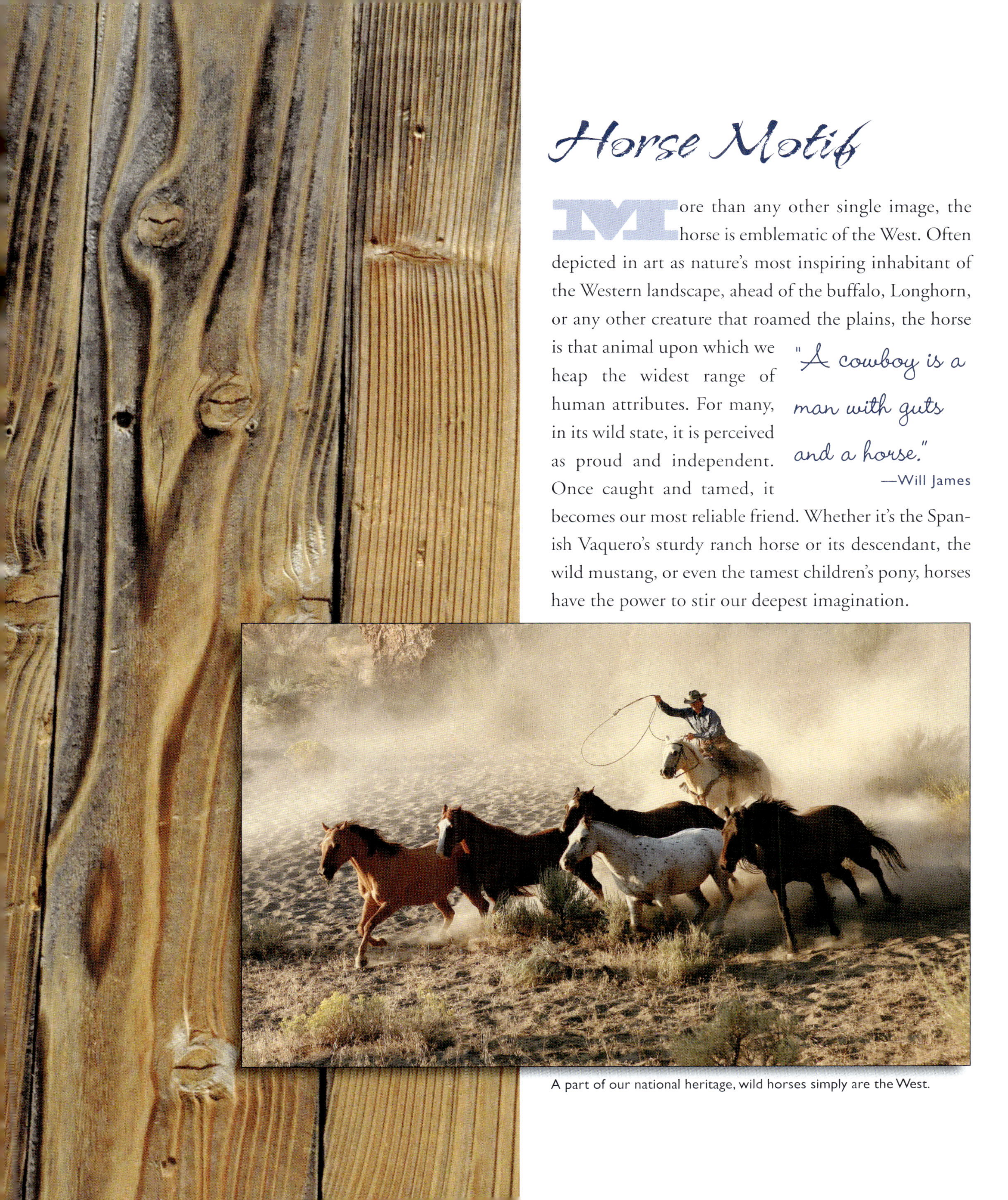

Horse Motif

More than any other single image, the horse is emblematic of the West. Often depicted in art as nature's most inspiring inhabitant of the Western landscape, ahead of the buffalo, Longhorn, or any other creature that roamed the plains, the horse is that animal upon which we heap the widest range of human attributes. For many, in its wild state, it is perceived as proud and independent. Once caught and tamed, it becomes our most reliable friend. Whether it's the Spanish Vaquero's sturdy ranch horse or its descendant, the wild mustang, or even the tamest children's pony, horses have the power to stir our deepest imagination.

"A cowboy is a man with guts and a horse."
—Will James

A part of our national heritage, wild horses simply are the West.

Horse motif airbrush stencil. Simple and spectacular in my eyes—an understated design. Adobeware by Syracuse China, 1955.

Above: The spectacular platter measuring 14 inches is probably the showstopper of my personal collection—my very favorite piece. Created by Paul Davidson for "Winchester '73," the motif is a masterful drawing, hand-colored under the glaze.

Right: Back in the 1950s, travelers could send post cards like these back home to the folks. What better way to say, "We're out West!"

One of the most frequent depictions on dinnerware over time has been the bucking bronco, an animal whose power, strength, and defiance seem to capture the hearts of all. Immortalized on canvas, sculpted in bronze, and brought to life in literature, it's not surprising that numerous examples of Western-themed dinnerware include his image.

In fact, the horse has reared, galloped, and bucked his way across tableware for years. Some depictions have shown him unsaddled, others tacked up and ready to work, often with a cowboy or cowgirl mounted up. In the folklore of the American West, yesterday as today, the horse has proved to be a cowboy's essential companion.

With hopes for the preservation and protection of the horse in the wild, this magnificent animal will continue to stand for the West and our collective dream of freedom.

A good horse is never a bad color."

—Anonymous

Alert and reliable, there's nothing like a good ranch horse. Dry Creeks Rodeo, Springfield, Colorado. Courtesy Tabitha Smith.

Cowboy Hat Motif

The ten-gallon hat is, without question, a universal symbol of the American cowboy. Famed Americans wore cowboy hats, including Teddy Roosevelt, Buffalo Bill Cody, John Wayne, Jimmy Stewart, and of course Roy Rogers. The hat was not only a piece of headgear, but since the golden age of Western movies it was often inferred that the wearer belonged to a certain culture with a clear value set—a follower of the Cowboy Code, a man with honor and integrity. The mere tipping of a hat denoted respect and friendship. As early as the 1940s, Hollywood helped the viewer discern who was who in the various B Westerns—white hats were the good guys, black hats weren't.

"A man isn't a man without a Stetson."

—"Put" Putney, Texas Ranger

The technique of airbrush design has a long history. It's a wonderful application when used with a stencil on dinnerware, as seen here in this stunning plate by Syracuse China, circa 1950s, one from a decorative collection featuring hats and saddles.

Classy handmade cowboy hats can be had for the discerning customer. These two examples are by Colorado's own Greeley Hat Works, Trent L. Johnson, hatter. Brown hat—Cattleman's style with cutter bumps; Fawn color hat—Classic Gus style. (Courtesy Trent Johnson)

This handsome plate shows the modern day cowboy in action with a nicely drawn hat bordered by twisted barbed wire. Plate by Sonoma Lifestyles "Happy Trails." Spurs courtesy Jackie Bell, Hampden Equestrian, Lakewood, CO.

Back in 1865, hatter John B. Stetson improved the flat-brimmed style of hat brought from the East, and made it more popular with cowboys. The hat body was constructed of beaver fur felt and had a large crown and a wide, heavily starched and ironed brim to protect the wearer from the sun and rain. It was durable and held up in all kinds of weather. So successful was this design with cattlemen and cowboys that it became hugely popular across the frontier. Referred to as "The Boss of the Plains," it's still being made today, though worn mostly by nostalgia buffs and reenactors.

The best of today's cowboy hats are made of a variety of materials, including fur felt and various types of grasses or straw. Not surprisingly, dinnerware artists have often drawn the style of hat that was popular at the time—it's fascinating to look at the various depictions over time and see how the fashion changes. Of course, certain styles of hats are more popular in certain geographic regions: flat-brimmed and flat-crowned styles, for example, versus a peaked crown and a curled brim. A buckaroo from Idaho might wear a very different shape of hat than would a cowboy from Oklahoma.

Various forms of cowboy hats show up on plates as center motifs, as well as border designs. No image of a cowboy on a horse in my personal china collection is shown without one. Nor are any of them shown wearing a close fitting brimmed cap (ball cap), a very common and very twenty-first century convenience.

Cowboys in straw hats at Dry Creeks Rodeo, Springfield, Colorado, summer 2009. Ranch rodeo team, "The Regulators": Clint Plagge, left; Ryan Bulkley, center; Howdy Huffman, right. (Courtesy Tabitha Smith)

Boots and Spurs Motif

Boots

Cowboy boots have been reported to have the amazing ability to transform most wearers instantly from an everyday person into a true Western galoot. (That's cowboy talk for "wrangler," and everyone I know who's ever donned a pair of cowboy boots confirms it.) The mere act of putting on a pair of this flattering footwear makes a person feel more attractive, act more courageous, and yearn for a horse.

Some boots have wide, flat heels and are made for walking or doing

"Boots don't actually make a man look taller, they make him think taller."
—C.J. Brown

Canyon Ranch Collection by Home Studio, distributed by Kohl's. Stoneware dinner plate in vitreous light blue glaze with stars on "denim" rim. Hand-painted and made in China, circa 2005.

Vintage examples of exceptional boots, thanks to the Justin Boot Company. The Champion boot is from the 1940s, and the Eagle boot is from the mid-1960s. Some things just get better with time. (Courtesy French | West | Vaughan for Justin Boots) Right: Airbrushed stencil design by Jackson China, 1950s–'60s. Brown glaze on white glaze, airbrushed rim and stencil.

ranch chores; others are higher and narrower and have a deep slant. Some are almost knee high with finger-pull holes for pulling them on. Others are shorter and barely cover the ankle. Whatever the style, be they inlaid, tooled, stitched, or plain, Western boots are a palette for the bootmaker's art. Every era produced a different variation, and so it continues today, but the basic concept of footwear made for riding stays the same. A cowboy just wouldn't be a cowboy without them.

Western dinnerware artists loved them, too, as a wonderful opportunity for decoration and self-expression.

Spurs

Like jewelry on the perfect outfit, the spur can be a spectacular addition to the cowboy's wardrobe—except that it's more than decorative, it's designed with a purpose. Forged of metal and often silver-plated, plain, stamped, or engraved, the spur was designed to rest on the back of the boot heel and aid in communication with a horse. The mere touch of a spur is usually all a horse needs to know where the rider is and what he or she wants. A well-trained horse can feel the edge of a rowel and respond instantly.

Oversized grill plate with center bronco and right and left spurs. white glaze on pottery. Made in Japan circa 1950s by Fred Roberts Company, USA.

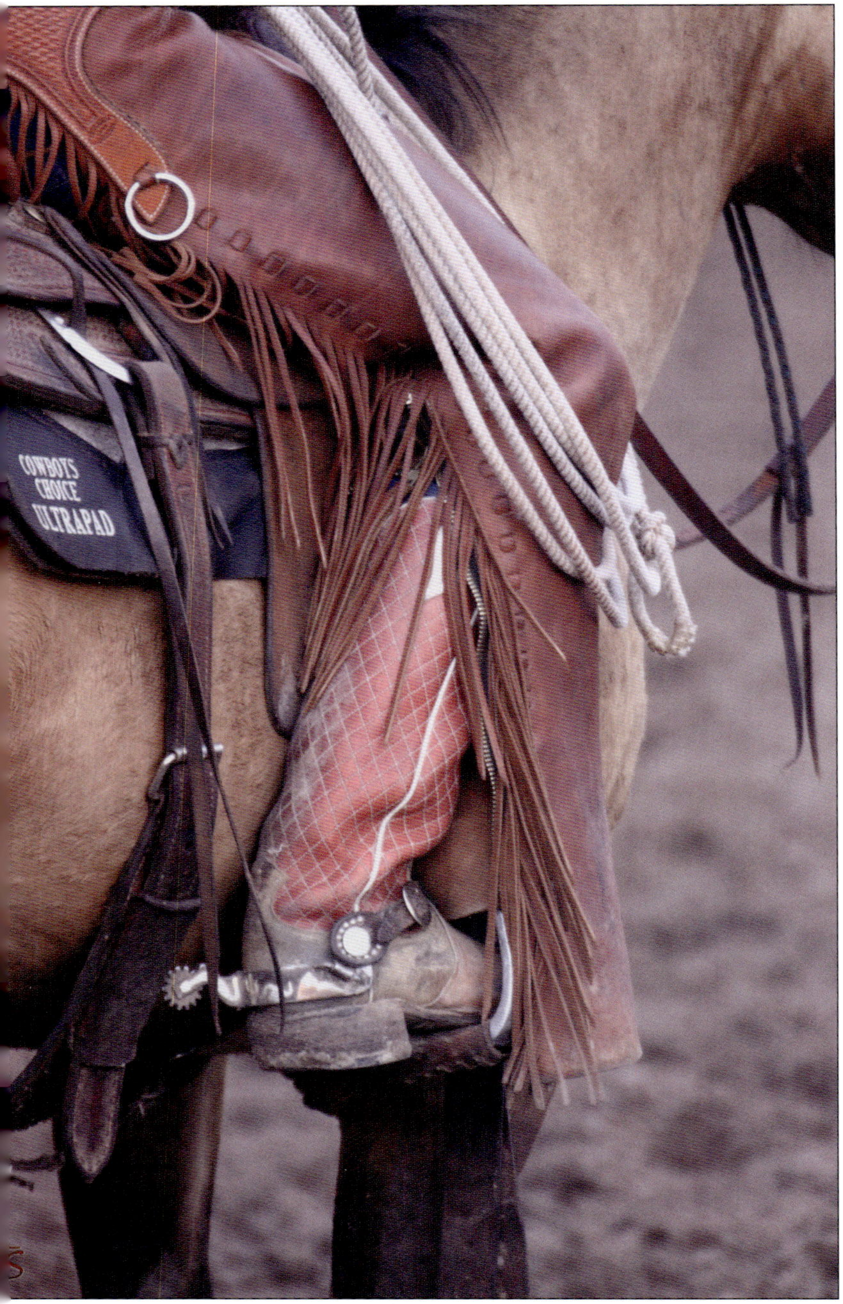

Rodeo cowboys use spurs to "rake" or touch the horse on the shoulder, a very different kind of application. Points on the rowels are flattened so as not to hurt the animal's skin.

No one knows exactly when spurs were first created, but indications are that as far back as 1000 A.D., the Roman mounted legions used them. They've also been found in the artifacts of the cavalries of Asia's Genghis Kahn. Today, spurs have come to be a part of every discipline's riding gear, English or Western. Spanish explorers brought the large, fancy roweled version first to Mexico and then into this country. Our modern day Western spurs have evolved from there.

> *"A man who wears spurs has high expectations; a woman who wears spurs has a mind of her own."*
>
> —Anonymous

Today, most spurs are less obtrusive and smaller in scale, fabricated in a mix of decorative metals. As collectible as they are beautiful, they add the richness of the metal smith and engraver's art to Western gear. Many spurs are personalized and become family heirlooms. And of course, dinnerware artists have added them to their iconography in great detail.

Above: Boot with spur. Dry Creeks Rodeo in Springfield, Baca County, Colorado, 2009. (Courtesy Tabitha Smith)
Right: Top-of-the-line handmade spurs by Tom Balding, Sheridan, Wyoming. Antique brown finish with sterling engraved bars on shanks. (Courtesy Tom Balding)

Saddle Motif

Tepco China: Handsome dinner plate with saddle in center, part of "Branding Irons" series, 1940s and '50s.

The West couldn't have been tamed without a horse, nor the horse tamed without a saddle. More than just a seat to keep the rider mounted, the saddle is a working cowboy's best tool, designed to keep a man comfortable on a horse for hours at a time with an all-essential horn around which a rope can wind (or dally) when needed. With several hundred pounds of steer on the other end, a good saddle not only had to be sturdy enough to hold a rope but withstand plenty of pressure in every direction, too. It was also home to a man's rain slicker, bedroll, and rifle.

Vintage saddle made for rodeo personality Kitty Canutt by Hamley's Saddlery, 1940s. (Courtesy of Hamley and Company, established 1883, Pendleton, Oregon)

A very good saddle was handmade back then, and still is today, designed in any one of several popular styles that suit the kind of work a cowboy does. Mass-produced or production line saddles are the other choice, where each step of the construction process is performed by a different person.

Two clearly identifiable styles have evolved from the early days: the Buckaroo or slick fork style, known as the "Californio," and the "Texican," or swell fork, square-skirt style saddle. Each is designed for strength, durability, and comfort. Numerous variations have evolved based on the intended use of the saddle, as applied to cutting, barrel racing, reining, or riding Western pleasure.

"If the saddle don't fit, change horses."

—C.J. Brown

If done well, a saddle is a beautiful thing to behold, solid of tree and graceful of decoration, from pommel to cantle, some with fully carved stirrup leathers and covered stirrups as well. A Mexican saddle might have a wide round roping pommel and elongated *tapaderos,* or covers, to protect the rider's feet. A proud tradition throughout the West, the making of saddles has become a fine art.

According to the Hamley Saddlery in Pendleton, Oregon, following the 1919 Pendleton Round-Up, rodeo organizers from around the region agreed that a standard bronc saddle must be used in all rodeo competitions. They developed the modified Association saddle as a solution to give every rider the same advantage.

Till Goodan design for Wallace China, 1950s, "Boots & Saddle" collection. (Courtesy True West Home)

This same style of saddle is used today in pro-rodeo saddle bronc events.

China manufacturers like Tepco celebrated the saddle in the 1950s with a distinctive line drawing that must have thrilled a cowboy's heart. Texas artist Buckeye Blake created an image for Pipestone in the 1990s in four colors—bold, crisp, and bright. California artist Till Goodan immortalized the saddle in his famous "Boots & Saddle" pattern for Wallace China in warm shades of brown and tan. A future generation of china designers might prove that perhaps the best saddle motif is yet to come.

A masterful job creating the effect of saddle and skirt via airbrush. Syracuse China, circa 1950s.

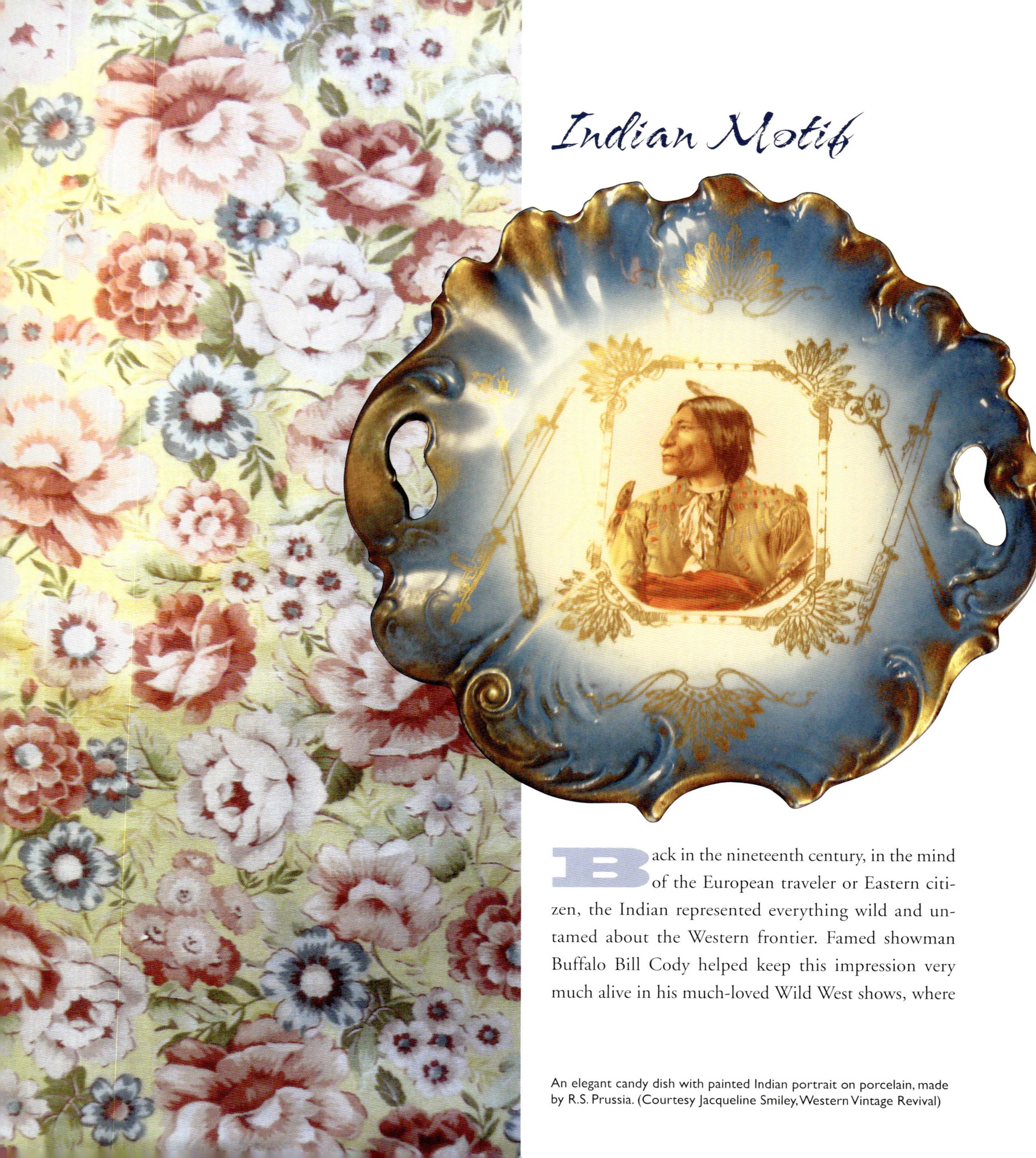

Indian Motif

Back in the nineteenth century, in the mind of the European traveler or Eastern citizen, the Indian represented everything wild and untamed about the Western frontier. Famed showman Buffalo Bill Cody helped keep this impression very much alive in his much-loved Wild West shows, where

An elegant candy dish with painted Indian portrait on porcelain, made by R.S. Prussia. (Courtesy Jacqueline Smiley, Western Vintage Revival)

Indians appeared before live audiences, replaying historic events. In what was the most popular of acts, the legendary Lakota warrior Yellow Hand reenacted his attack on Buffalo Bill. Fortunately, both survived—to thunderous applause.

It's no wonder dinnerware artists sought the image of the Indian. Collector plates and everyday service showed his portrait or silhouette. Other popular mediums of the day, like postcards and dude ranch brochures, showed chieftains in full regalia. Indians were a popular merchandising image that Americans and foreigners couldn't resist.

The Indian image began to fade as a decorative element by the 1960s, when a growing sense of political awareness began to shape our depictions of minorities, and Indians especially. One of the last commercial appearances on china turned up on a vintage cup from the 1980s with a bronc buster on one side and a mounted Indian on the other, depicted in hot pursuit, lance poised, headdress feathers flying.

Top: For a period in our history, a chieftain astride his horse in full war bonnet was the heroic image of a Native American. Left: The scalloped rim gives this plate a special refinement. Indian profile against rising thunderhead clouds, highly glazed vitreous restaurant china by Sterling China, circa 1950s.

Left: Yet another depiction of Native America, a postcard once popular among Western tourist stops, circa 1950.
Below: This piece of Syracuse china was possibly made for a restaurant, hotel, or train service. Its origins are a mystery.

Hartstone Pottery's "Sky Ranch" series released a lyrical drawing of an Indian brave seated next to his horse in the 1980s, but very few other representations have shown up in my collecting efforts since that time.

By the time the Indian image on Western dinnerware had disappeared, a different kind of reference appeared in the form of Native American art as applied to everyday products. The Pendleton Company, long committed to the creation of blankets woven to sell to

Top: A bold return to Native America and the mythic warrior, circa 1990. Note the floral motif—a real beauty, by Michelle & Company.
Above: "Bits of the Southwest" by Vernon Kilns, circa 1960s. A beautiful depiction of an Indian with his pueblo in the distance.

Inspired by the ledger art of the Plains Indians, these running horses have a thoroughly modern feel. This platter hangs on the wall, a piece of vibrant ceramic art. Pendleton Home Collection.

Native American tribes of the North and Southwest, put specially researched designs on colorful mugs based on five of their legendary blanket patterns. These were the start of a new ceramic tableware collection that debuted in 2001, and later added brilliant patterns on dinnerware and accessories as well.

A book such as this cannot overlook the highly geometric and whimsical images of Mimbres art as it appears on work produced by Pipestone. Pipestone is one of several companies over the years that has carried on

Mimbreno Pottery

As explained in *Mimbres Pottery, Ancient Art of the American Southwest,* by Hudson Hill Press and the American Arts Federation, the Classic Mimbres culture thrived from 1000 to the early 1150s, occupying a 46-mile valley in southwestern New Mexico, an area watered by streams and rich with wildlife. Their isolated culture lasted some 150 years and differed from other farming cultures of New Mexico in the development of sophisticated pottery. Notably, highly ornamental clay bowls were found in excavations placed over the heads of the deceased. These were decorated with birds, animals, and fish, ranging from the simple to the ornate, all depicting the world of nature.

Mimbres is Spanish for "willow," a tree of the region. No one knows what these people called themselves. Some 2,000 samples of their art fills museums and private collections, fueling a movement to preserve their ancestral home.

Above: Hand-painted reproduction Mimbres pottery, "Waterbirds," from Pipestone.

Demitasse cup from the Pipestone collection of "Mimbreno" dinnerware.

the tradition of restaurant china originally produced for the Santa Fe Railway. The design was developed by designer/architect Mary Elizabeth Jane Colter, and made for the Santa Fe Railway by Syracuse China. The dinnerware was created specifically for the railroad's newest train at the time, the Super Chief, a line with a diesel engine and a new streamlined look. It had picture windows, air-conditioning, elegant interiors, and consisted of five Pullman cars, a diner, and a lounge car. The interiors were decorated in the Southwestern tradition.

Ms. Colter was chief architect and decorator for the Fred Harvey Company from 1902 to 1948. She was also a brilliant designer with a vision based on restoring Southwestern cultural influences in architecture, particularly at the Grand Canyon. According to Virginia L. Grattan, author of the essential biography *Mary Colter: Builder Upon the Red Earth*, the project began this way:

"For the tableware of the Fred Harvey diners, Colter wanted something that was very distinctive. Indian art, yet something unique. In southern New Mexico, archeologists had recently unearthed one-thousand-year-old pottery of the Mimbreno Indians. Colter decided to reproduce designs from this ancient pottery on the new china. She had her secretary, Sadie Rubins, contact the major museums to gather information about the Mimbreno, and after thorough study Colter created thirty-seven different decorations for the various pieces of china. She used not only the formal patterns, but also the simple designs of birds, animals, and fish, produced in a rose hue on light tan pottery . . . Colter designed the silver service and flatware as well, making the table settings on this modern dining car a reminder of the antiquity and its art."

New designers emerge even today throughout the West, such as Native American potter Greystone Abbott, Cherokee Bird Clan, who resides in Colorado (see page 220). She creates distinctive handmade dinnerware sets with images from her Cherokee tradition.

Brand Motif

Branding was an essential element to the development of the cattle trade in the American West. Without it, cattle that intermingled on the open range couldn't be identified. Horses were branded too, and in this modern-day era of alternate identification methods like microchips or freeze brands, brands are still a common method for keeping track of one's stock.

"A brand gives a cow a home to belong to."
—C.J. Brown

Airbrushed saucer by Jackson China, Falls Creek, Pennsylvania. Back stamp reads "Jac Tan," a type of restaurant ware, early 1950s.

Even after the invention of barbed wire, the open range still persisted in places, and many ranches let their herds run together, sorting them out only at round-up. A brand was the only means of claiming ownership. The custom of branding dates as far back as the Egyptians and has evolved over time. It takes skill and precision, plus the right timing, to make a brand that just sears the skin, without submitting the animal to injury or over-scarring. Brands unfortunately could be altered by rustlers or cattle thieves and often were, causing a special branch of stock detectives to be created as far back as the nineteenth century—men whose jobs were to protect the rancher in a challenging industry.

The lexicon of brands is an alphabet or language all by itself. Brands are read from left to right and from top to bottom. Any combination of alphabet letters, numbers, slashes, half circles, crosses, and bars could be used. The elements could be shown reversed, hanging (below one another) or simply drawn like a pictograph, such as a ladder or a rising sun.

Dinnerware artists have utilized the decorative aspects of the brand in countless ways. In the 1940s and '50s, Artist Till Goodan used brands of real ranches on all his plates for Wallace, and even went so far as to provide a small brand identification booklet with every set.

Some artists never did their homework, combining a mixture of brand-like symbols and pawning them off as the real thing. One series with no back stamp, but reportedly made for Sears in the 1970s, has been sold as a

Vintage brand brochure from Wallace China, a guide to enjoying a Wallace purchase, circa 1950s. The codex lists all the ranches and the brands. (Courtesy Betty Goodan Andrews, author's collection)

Western brand plate in spite of the fact that most of these symbols are merely astrological signs!

When it comes to Western dinnerware, the decorative qualities of the brand as a border or overall motif show up repeatedly throughout the decades. For new collectors, they just might be the first tip that the item you've found has a touch of Western flair and might be something of value.

Brand plate—or maybe not. Although this plate was purchased from a reputable dealer who sells Western collectibles on the Internet, it appeared undecipherable to me upon arrival. Closer inspection by the National Cowboy and Western Heritage Museum Curator of Cowboy Culture, Don Reeves, proved that most of the images aren't brands at all. It's easy for us greenhorns to be fooled.

A-1—Flying A brand of Gene Autry, famous Motion Picture and Radio star. Ranches at San Fernando, Calif., and Gene Autry, Okla.
A-2—One-O-One. Famous wild west show outfit, with headquarters in Oklahoma. Also used by Sam White of Pixley, California.
A-3—Z Slash D. Brand of Porters, Arizona, famous makers of saddles and cowboy equipment.
A-4—Seventy-Six. Noted Arizona outfit.
A-5—Twenty-Five. Well known Nevada brand in use for more than seventy-five years.
A-6—Cross & Crescent. Rancho El Tejon. One of the largest in California, extending from the Mojave Desert across the Tehachapi Mountains to the San Joaquin Valley.
A-7—Double X connected. Registered in California by the Field family for three generations.
A-8—Lazy S J—Cattle brand of Ralph Jones, Porterville, California.
A-9—Conrad Kohr—A pioneer Montana brand.
A-10—J Four. Brand of Will Rogers' father. Registered in Oklahoma.
B-1—Diamond A. Boquillos Land & Cattle Co., with ranches in New Mexico, Arizona and California.
B-2—O Bar O. Famous old New Mexico ranch. Once the hide-out of Billy, the Kid, notorious outlaw credited with killing twenty-one men before he was twenty-one years of age. The Kid was killed by Pat Garrett, sheriff of Lincoln County, New Mexico.
B-3—Box Y. A noted Texas outfit.
B-4—Bell Ranch. One of the greatest cattle ranches of New Mexico.
B-5—R A Connected. Rancho Antero. Brand of Roy Nafziger, Colorado.
B-6—Circle A. Official State brand of Arizona.
B-7—Lone Star. Official State brand of Texas.
B-8—T O. Santa Margarita Rancho, San Diego County, California. The largest old Spanish Land Grant still intact.
B-9—Seven X L. Wyoming brand of Senator Warren.
B-10—Three Feathers. Canadian ranch of the Prince of Wales.
C-1—Bar W. New Mexico brand of Governor Lew Wallace, author of Ben Hur.
C-2—Pitchfork. One of the greatest of old Texas outfits.
C-3—Square and Compass. The first brand registered in Montana.
C-4—Running W. The great King ranch of Texas. Largest in the United States, covering 1,250,000 acres. Also the California brand of Louis Wulfekuhler.
C-5—Rocking F. Montana brand of Will James, famous cowboy author and artist.
C-6—Quarter Circle X. Cattle and horse brand of Dean McComber, Rancho Rio Vista, Springville, California. Also owner of Broken Bar Pack Outfit and Camp Nelson Resort.
C-7—Forty Five. Brand once used by Walter Greig Pack Outfit, Quaking Aspen Meadows, California.
C-8—H B Conected. Brand of Roy Boone and Walter Huston, famous actor of stage, screen and radio. Ranch located at Glenville, California.
C-9—Wrangles Roost Dude Ranch, Phoenix, Ariz.
C-10—Sahuaro Lake Dude Ranch, Mesa Arizona.
D-1—Cross Triangle Dude Ranch, Prescott, Ariz.
D-2—L U Bar Guest Ranch. Located in Wind River Mountains, Dubois, Wyoming.
D-3—Two N Dude Ranch, Dubois, Wyoming.
D-4—Allan Guest Ranch, Augusta, Montana.
D-5—Seven Eleven Guest Ranch. In the Gallatin National Forest, Gallatin Gateway, Mont.
D-6—Lazy J P Conected. Famous old time Idaho brand.
D-7—Pine View Dude Ranch. Located on the Blackfoot River near Soda Springs, Idaho.
D-8—Robinson Bar Dude Ranch. Salmon River Mountains, Clayton, Idaho.
D-9—U S Bar Guest Ranch, Ukiaha, Oregon.
D-10—S L W Guest Ranch, Greeley, Colorado. A pioneer cattle and horse ranch once owned by Lord Ogilvy, one of Colorado's most colorful figures.
E-1—Bar S Guest Ranch, Evergreen, Colorado.
E-2—Al Bar. Bolderado Guest Ranch. One of the oldest ranches in Nevada. Located near Las Vegas.
E-3—T H Guest Ranch, Sutcliffe, Nevada.
E-4—B Bar H Dude Ranch. In the Coachella Valley, Garnet, California.

Jackson China, Falls Creek, Pennsylvania, circa 1950s. Creamer with brand. Matches dinner plate on page xi.

Longhorns and Other Cattle Motif

Some say the history of the West wouldn't be what it is without the Longhorn. A formidable breed of cattle, the spread of this wily animal from Mexico through Texas and onto the Great Plains shaped cowboy culture like nothing else.

As the railroads came West, towns sprang up, communities needed to be fed, and eastern cities clamored for beef. Rounding up feral cattle and establishing ranches defined range life for almost half a century. The growth of the railroad and the arrival of the homesteader eventually prohibited trail drives of mammoth herds to railheads for shipment to slaughterhouses, and the industry turned to fenced ranching and feedlots instead.

Above Left: This bull appears to own the Texas plains. (Courtesy Tim O'Byrne, photographer and editor, *Working Ranch* magazine). Above: Red Angus—Colorado beef cattle grazing at the American Ranch at Sandstone, Larkspur, Colorado.

"A slice of cow is worth 8 cents in the cow, 14 cents in the hands of the packers, and $2.50 in a restaurant that specializes in atmosphere."

—Joe Evans, El Paso, Texas, 1939

Homer Laughlin china, "Rhythm," circa 1954. An amazing adaptation of a roping cowboy to the side of a cup!

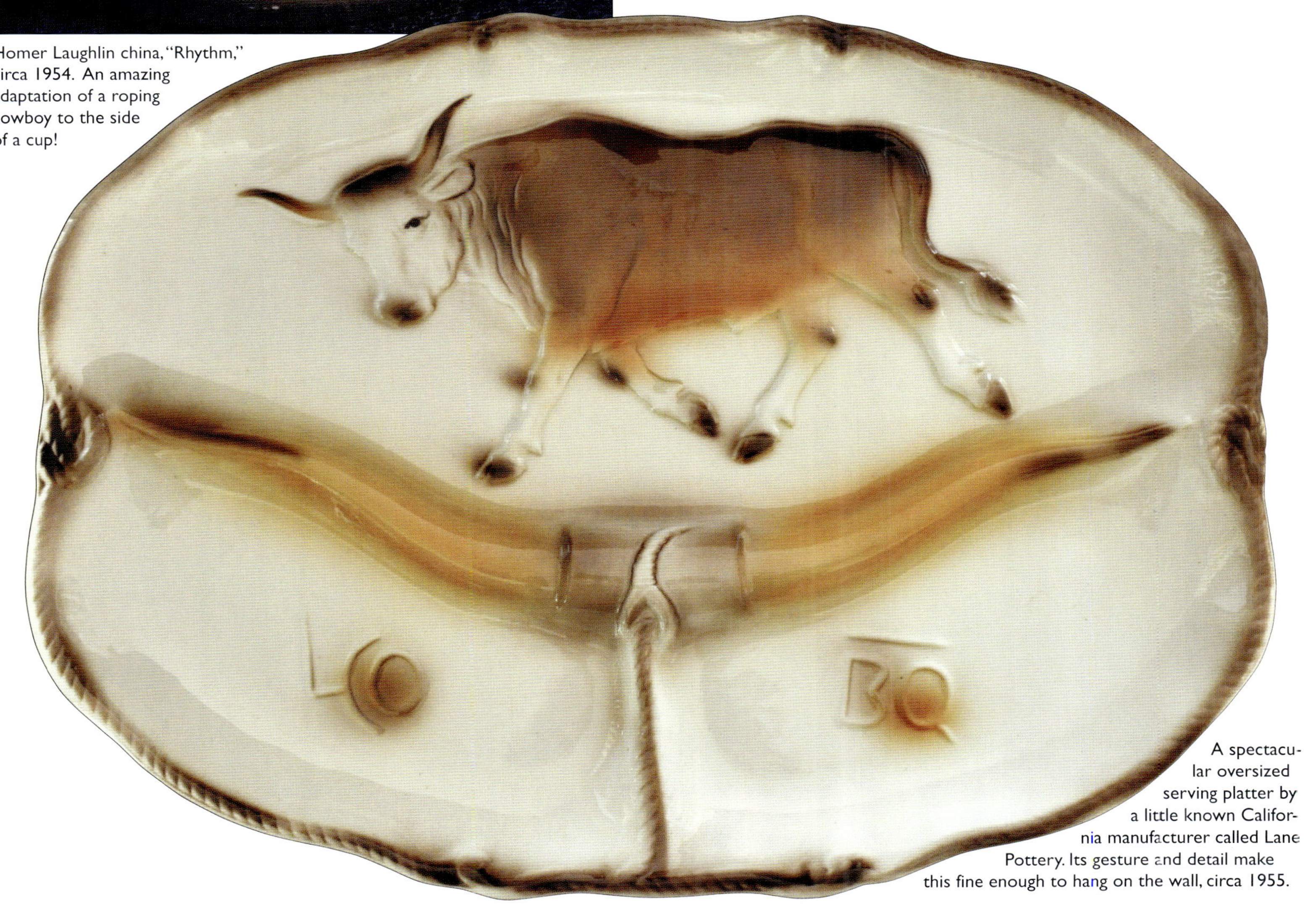

A spectacular oversized serving platter by a little known California manufacturer called Lane Pottery. Its gesture and detail make this fine enough to hang on the wall, circa 1955.

Man's relationship with bovines goes back to an era long before recorded time. The first animals to be domesticated in Europe were a type of early oxen or its relatives like the Highland cattle of Scotland. With those pioneers who opened the West came Englishmen and Scotsmen who brought various breeds from the English Isles and were adept at raising them. By the 1870s, after populating the Great Plains, the Longhorns gave way to a cow that could be milked as well as produce beef, and imported breeds of short-horned cattle replaced the huge free-roaming herds.

By the 1880s, over 250 ranches under Scottish and English deed could be found in Colorado and Wyoming, and investor-run ranches flooded the prairies with livestock. The Hereford, the prized red and white cow of England, and later the red or black Angus, were favored. Later still, assorted

Left: "Running Longhorns," an original watercolor by Eve Armson for Cowboy Living's "Classic West" collection.
Above: The simplicity of this striking heavy porcelain bull head by Stillmeadow Pottery gives this plate real class, circa 1980s.

breeds like the French Charolais and the Brahma were introduced. Smaller breeds like the Coriente from Mexico became popular, as well. A variety of cross-breeds began to surface as ranchers sought hardier meat producers and more competitive stock.

The history of the West is the cattleman's story of survival. Populations here and abroad depended on food, and America provided beef for its own tables and those of Europe. Unlike anything back East, the Western plains were covered with an abundance of short grasses like gramma and buffalo, sand blue stem and wheat grass, all hardy and nourishing. Ranching remains the mainstay of many rural populations across the Western states.

"Head 'Em Up—Move 'Em Out ..."

—Eric Fleming as Gil Favor, Trailboss on TV's *Rawhide*

Western dinnerware artists have not ignored this subject, from the feisty Longhorn to the short-horned breeds, especially the endearing white-faced Hereford. Although their images are

Jackson and Syracuse China, circa 1960s.

"Classic West" collection by Cowboy Living. Durable porcelain for everyday use. Metal chargers also available in round or oval shape. Original watercolors by Eve Armson.

less popular today than in yesteryear, china collectors can still find many diverse examples honoring the breeds that are at the heart of the West.

Round-Up, the Real Story

If you've never headed out into the brush on the back of a horse in search of a mama cow and her calf, you've missed something. Imagine the cool crisp air of early morning, the intoxicating smell of mesquite or sage, and the extra sense of excitement and anticipation in the horse beneath you, ready to break into a lope, or let loose an extra crow hop or buck just for the fun of it.

That herd ahead, which you're helping to move to fenced pasture, to new grazing ground, or toward a temporary corral to be separated, branded, and let loose again, is watching you, and starting to move. That's thousands of pounds of raw, unpredictable energy on the hoof.

Whatever the reason, and whatever your role, you're part of a time-honored tradition, repeated spring and fall, one that clearly tests a horse's mettle and a cowboy's skill. One never knows when a steer might make a break, deciding to head back to where you found it, or when an ornery bunch might straggle off to go their own way. Quick reflexes and a good rope are the only recourse. Keeping a herd quiet and moving together is the best hope. Not losing a single critter is essential.

Vernon Kilns, Longhorn round-up detail on large platter, from "Winchester '73" collection. (Courtesy Janet Hix)

Sometimes it's necessary to leave a cow behind. If she doesn't have her calf, it's essential to let her go back and find it. She'll either catch up the next day or the cowboys will return and gather her up on the re-ride. A re-ride, or "straggling," always takes place after a gather. The crew goes in and makes the gather and then a few days later the boss will send one or two guys back to canvass that same area. Any cows that were missed are usually pretty lonesome by then and they'll show up, curious and ready to follow. They might be those odd steers that didn't want to be found (older steers and heifers, some bulls, or that, odd cranky, wild cow), but they all share one idea—they don't want to be left alone.

The challenge of the round-up embraces the very essence of ranching—man versus animal, requiring a mixture of courage, patience, and respect. It's a job that at one time, long before fences, was done on a very grand scale—a difficult job that had to be done. Rounding up hundreds of cows and holding them together was something only the best crew could muster.

Today, ranchers still have to move their herds. Maybe not so many nor so far. But as long as the West exists, there'll be cattle to gather—even, as some cowboys put it, until that last round-up in the sky. It's not surprising that the subject of a round-up, of either cattle or horses, has been approached by artists in both two- and three-dimensional media. What is astonishing is that it has found its way onto a dinner plate, as well.

Rodeo Motif

"Saddle Up" offset lithograph. Original mixed media by artist Tandi Venter, Parker, Colorado. (Courtesy Encore Art Group)

Across the United States and western Canada, the spectacle of rodeo unites cowboy culture. The pairing of man against beast in a series of events designed to show off riding skill, precision, and coordination between mounted horsemen (as in team roping), and the exhibition of sheer guts and bravado is simply unbeatable. It's actually the official sport of Texas and Wyoming.

The rodeo has come a long way from the days when cowboys gathered informally to exhibit the skills needed to herd cattle. The great rodeos, which

Frontier Days champion bucking horse vintage photo. (Courtesy Cheyenne Frontier Days Rodeo)

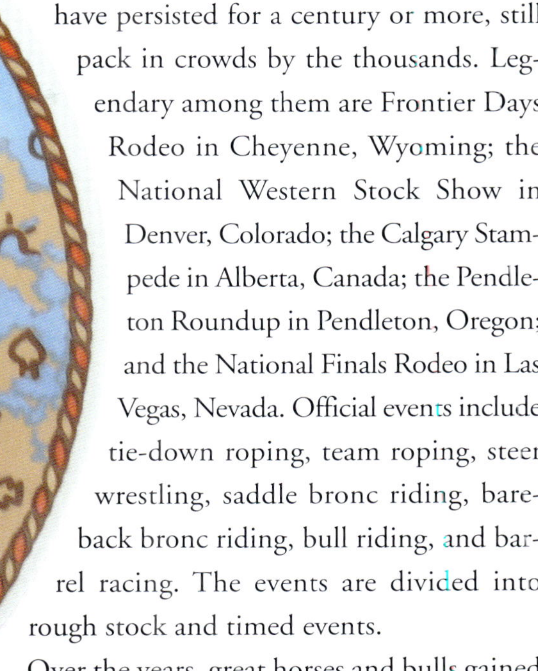

have persisted for a century or more, still pack in crowds by the thousands. Legendary among them are Frontier Days Rodeo in Cheyenne, Wyoming; the National Western Stock Show in Denver, Colorado; the Calgary Stampede in Alberta, Canada; the Pendleton Roundup in Pendleton, Oregon; and the National Finals Rodeo in Las Vegas, Nevada. Official events include tie-down roping, team roping, steer wrestling, saddle bronc riding, bareback bronc riding, bull riding, and barrel racing. The events are divided into rough stock and timed events.

Over the years, great horses and bulls gained reputations as great as the cowboys who rode them. The champion cowboys showed the rest of the country what it took to stay in the arena, some far beyond their years considering the abuse that bronc and bull riding does to the body. Legendary competitors like Jim Shoulders, Casey Tibbs, Dan Mortensen, Larry Mahan, Ty Murray, and Trevor Brazile are revered names in the West, giants in the arena.

"It takes a lot of courage for a man to pay out his dollar to enter a rodeo and then, after not winning a red cent, walk away saying, 'Sure lucky I didn't get hurt.'" —Hoot Gibson, Hollywood, 1912

Top: Bold image by Buckeye Blake for Pipestone, a contemporary approach to the subject, yet rooted in the tradition. A special design that stands alone. Left: This marvelous drawing for Sky Ranch by Hartstone captures the speed and power required to turn barrels on a horse and completes the shape of the bowl perfectly.

Women competed in rodeo, too, through the early 1920s when they were allowed to ride rough stock just as men riders did, and a bevy of hardy cowgirls wowed fans like no other time in history. Trick riders, sharp shooters, bronc busters, and Roman riders—they could do it all. That is, until famed cowgirl and bronc rider Bonnie McCarroll was killed in an arena in 1929—thrown from her horse and trampled—a tragedy that changed rodeo for women forever. In the highly regulated world of the Professional Cowboy Rodeo Association and the Women's Pro Rodeo Association, women are now restricted to safer sports like barrel racing and pole bending.

Dinnerware designers seem to love bronc busters. The Pendleton Woolen Mills has chosen to put the famed "Let 'Er Buck" bronc emblem on a dinnerware pattern to commemorate their one-hundredth anniversary. This one image seems to say it all, recognizing both the strength of the horse and the cool of the cowboy to ride the storm through.

Right: Bulldogger: Till Goodan illustration for Wallace China, vintage 13-inch platter, circa 1950s, signed under the glaze.

Ranch Life Motif

Ranch life is both work and play, investment and reward. And ranchers love their lifestyle. In many ways, a sentimental pulse runs through popular Western art, as it should. After all, folks who love the West cherish their sense of community and family, relying on one another. Relationships are measured in years, not numbers. In small towns and wherever ranch life exists, often in remote areas, ranch folk celebrate together, grieve together, and pitch in when necessary to get the big jobs done. Important experiences are shared.

"Cherished," Paul Cameron Smith Collection for Montana Lifestyles, 2008. Wouldn't you love this romantic bowl at your place setting? Perfect for anniversary dinners.

Who says a simple photo can't be a successful image for dinnerware? This one by Randy Jay Braun for Rivers Edge speaks volumes. (2008)

Western art chronicles a unique way of life for others to enjoy. Many artists who design for the china medium have noted pastoral scenes and tender moments between families, lovers, and friends. How remarkable that even a dinner plate can remind us that life is made up of simple pleasures and enduring stories.

"The time to dance is when the music is playing ..."

—Unknown

I like to think of art as a response to external stimulus and/or internal feelings, a subject interpreted through the artist's eyes. In a commercial medium designed for home use, such as dinnerware, some of the humblest subjects have nonetheless been worthy of an artist's pen or brush. I see a humanity in this work that speaks of a cherished way of life, and values far beyond consumerism.

These enduring images, capturing special moments, add something extra to the simple grace of breaking bread, giving us a way to honor every meal.

"Ladies First," another charming reminder of growing up on a ranch. By Paul Cameron Smith for Montana Lifestyles. (2008)

Chuck Wagon Motif

Red Wing dinnerware. "Round-Up" pattern, dating from the 1960s. Hand-painted tableware for the home, breezy and modern in approach.

Back when Texas rancher and cattleman Charlie Goodnight, founder of the JA Ranch, invented the chuck wagon in 1866, no one ever dreamed that this kitchen and compact serving bar would become one of the most important components of Western frontier history.

The ingenious design with its multi-purpose pantry and drop-down work surface has survived time and use, as proven by the many fine old chuck wagons still in working order after providing victuals for over one hundred years. Across the West, chuck wagon cook-offs have become a huge favorite at Western festivals of all kinds.

During a cattle drive, the cow camp cook, or "cooky," stored foodstuffs, freshly killed game or butchered beef, tinned goods, flour, and spices inside the wagon bed, as well as kettles, pots, pans, and other cooking utensils. A wagon cover held high on curved hoops kept things dry and gave the cook room to organize. The back end of the wagon was a convenient storage system, with numerous drawers and cubbies for knives, spoons, and other cutlery, as well as essentials. Finally, the wagon's tailgate dropped down to form a table on which to prepare the food—usually freshly cooked baked beans, potatoes, roast meat, sour dough biscuits, and some kind of cobbler, all cooked in the hot coals of a fire, Dutch-oven style, and served of course, with cowboy coffee, hot and strong.

Woe to the cowboy who got too close to the "kitchen" while the cooky was setting things up. He'd be scuttled out of the

Soup bowl featuring Laton Huffman's vintage photo of a chuck wagon cook at work, circa 1900. By WesternWare Goods, Montana.

"A cowboy's recipe for coffee: Take one pound of coffee, wet it good with water, boil it for thirty minutes, pitch a horseshoe in, and if it sinks, put in some more coffee."

—Anonymous

Contents of a Chuck Wagon

In the wagon bed: bedrolls, slickers, wagon sheet, half-inch rope, guns, ammunition, lantern, kerosene, axle grease, extra wheel, salt pork, raw beef, green coffee beans, flour, sugar, salt, dried apples, onions, potatoes, grain for the work team.

In the tool box: shovel, ax, branding irons, horseshoeing equipment, hobbles, rods for a pot rack, extra skillets.

In the chuck box and boot: Flour, sugar, dried fruit, roasted coffee beans, pinto beans, plates, cups, cutlery, castor oil, calomel, bandages, thread, needle, razor and strop, salt, lard, baking soda, vinegar, chewing tobacco, rolling tobacco, sourdough, keg, matches, molasses, coffee pot, whiskey, skillets, Dutch ovens, pot hooks. Some also had a small cast iron oven and most had a water barrel.

—William H. Forbis
in *The Cowboys*

way with a whack. Each cowboy was expected to wait his turn, dish the food from the uncovered Dutch ovens onto his plate, then retire to a spot around the fire to enjoy the food on his own.

The dinnerware artists of the 1940s and '50s answered the call of backyard cooking by rendering the chuck wagon in countless ways. From manufacturers of enameled graniteware to hand-painted vitreous china or transferware, many have depicted this wonderful cow camp convenience.

Top: A vintage chuck wagon fully restored and in fine working order. Property of Daryl and Lisa Waite of the Withers Ranch, Hugo, Colorado. (Courtesy Michael Gamer)
Right: Just like the old days, sturdy wooden boxes hold implements. (Courtesy Michael Gamer)

Rifle and Revolver Motif

The West was a region where survival depended on courage, determination, and gunfire—and plenty of it. From the long rifles of the buffalo hunters to the six-shooters of the local sheriff and his armed deputies, the West was stocked with a variety of Winchesters, Colt single-action army "Peacemakers," Derringers, and even the mountain man's black powder muzzle loader. Game

Above: *Wanted Dead or Alive,* 1958–1961. Steve McQueen (Josh Randall) with his "mare's Laig" thrown over his shoulder. This series shot McQueen to super stardom, no pun intended. (Courtesy Bob Anderson, *Trail Dust* magazine)
Left: From the "Winchester '73" series by Vernon Kilns, possibly one of the finest Western designs to grace a dinner plate. Behind the rifle are archetypal Western scenes, covered wagon included. (Courtesy Janet Hix)

Casserole cover from Vernon Kilns' "Winchester '73" series. A pistol, gun belt, and holster—a rendering that's fresh and contemporary in design. Art by Paul Davidson. (Courtesy Janet Hix)

hunters favored the Sharps, a legendary buffalo gun, while mostly black powder rifles came West in wagon trains.

The U.S. Cavalry was armed, and the Native American warriors were armed as well, with weapons mostly acquired through trade or raids. Even the simple homesteader protected himself with a trusty rifle or sidearm. Out on the prairie, he might have perished from a deadly snake bite if he couldn't shoot the offending critter first. The traffic in arms was brisk, and it had to be in a land where a man often had to take justice into his own hands.

"A pair of six-shooters beats a pair of sixes."

—Belle Starr, 1887

Hollywood never let us forget that weapons ruled frontier life. The ring of gunfire or the volley of shots in an ambush or shoot-out, such as the one in the *The Shootout at the OK Corral,* peppered many films. *Winchester 73,* a film starring Jimmy Stewart and Shelly Winters, was named after the most popular model of rifle used in the old West. The importance of guns to the West hasn't been ignored by manufacturers of material culture. Even children's ceramic dinner sets sporting the likes of Roy Rogers and Hopalong Cassidy show them both brandishing six shooters.

One of my most unusual collector plates is a rendition of Mickey Mouse in a cowboy hat, circa 1960s, pointing a pistol astride his white horse (politically impossible today, no doubt).

Currently, 222 Fifth (PTS International), a modern-day china manufacturer, along with artist Kent Barton has turned the six-gun into a decorative border element on a dinner plate so benign the viewer hardly notices it. This, in turn, has become one of the favorite elements of specialty jewelry designer Jacqueline Smiley, who has incorporated the ceramic gun motif into her amazing necklace titled "Bad to the Bone."

As the decoration of Western dinnerware evolves, the appearance of rifles and revolvers will continue to occur, in some way reflecting the public's changing attitudes about them.

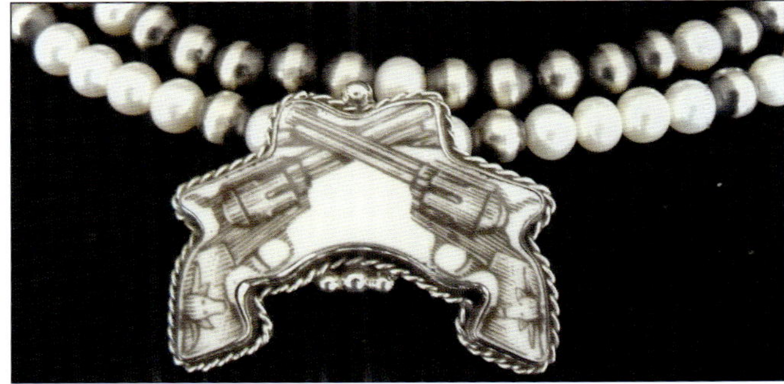

Top: "Two Gun Mickey" from 1968, series 1000, porcelain. Designed by Brenda White exclusively for the Walt Disney Company. Made in Japan. (Photo by Lindsay Allen)

Above: "Pistols and Pearls" necklace detail, stoneware and silver, silver beads and pearls. Beware the woman who can wear this necklace. She's someone to contend with—and proud of it! (Courtesy Western Vintage Revival)

Landscape Motif

Spacious grassland prairies, cactus-dotted deserts, wetlands, forests, and snow-covered mountains—the West is a changing landscape that dazzles the eye and the mind. Behind every scene of cowboys, cattle, or horses that has been drawn for a dinner plate is an implied vastness, if not a painted one. The art that's been selected connects with our preconceived ideas about the West and those impressions tap into a deeper need—to identify with that sense of place.

In some cases, as in the charming series done by Wellsville Pottery of Ohio, we're drawn straight into a Western town, that all too familiar "Main Street" that was often home to a brothel, a bank, a livery, and a saloon. The details on some plates are remarkable.

The "El Rancho" series by Wallace is stunning in that regard with its detailed Western scene. The implied landscape was approached by artist Till Goodan with "Pioneer Trails," and Tepco pulled it off in its Pony Express–themed "Western Traveler" dinnerware as well.

Created for the mass market rather than an elite few, these illustrations exceed the expected. There's no parallel in today's marketplace. I applaud the effort of any commercial artist who dared interpret the Western landscape on a dinner plate. That's true grit.

"The cow town has a mystique all its own. The word conjures up a vision of dusty streets, false-fronted buildings, hitching posts, cattle pens, railroad hacks, and innumerable mounted cowboys."
—Anonymous

Back stamp reads "Swingware" by Wellsville China of Ohio. One dealer titled the collection "Thirst Quench." Unfortunately, no history is available on this delightful rendering of a frontier town, part of a full table service including many serving pieces, circa 1950s to '70s.

Detail of Homer Laughlin "Rhythm" dinner plate with homestead scene. Makes you want to sing *Home on the Range*. See page 160.

Top: Yet another remarkable edition of the Old West remembered—the proverbial Main Street with open country and big sky beyond. By Wallace China, circa 1950s. (Photo by Lindsay Allen)
Above: Close-up of Main Street scene from "El Rancho" series by Wallace.
Right: Wallace China bread and butter plate, ranch with rider and hills beyond.

Cowboy Motif

"Saddle Up II," mixed media by Tandi Venter, Parker, Colorado (Courtesy Encore Art Group)

One can barely begin to separate the American cowboy, that hardworking individual who helps bring beef to the table, from the endless stories that surround him.

He's a man immortalized in literature and film as a true American hero—not for any single deed, but for successfully matching his skills against the land and the whims of nature, and succeeding in a way of life that has made quitters out of lesser men. Ranch hand or cattle baron, time has wrapped layers of history and myth around this one-time nomadic cow herder who for 150 years has helped tame the West.

Cowboy plate by Sterling. Back stamp reads "Desert Tan, Vitrified China, East Liverpool, Ohio. U.S.A." A romantic image of the lonely cowboy. Exact date unknown, circa 1950 or earlier.

Film scripts have placed him in dire straights and seen him triumph against all odds. The charms of women have gentled his nature and softened his heart, the wildest bulls and broncos have stomped his body into the dust, and the worst evils have challenged him to rise up for the cause of freedom and justice.

Bigger than life, the cowboy has become our greatest export after democracy, and the biggest proponent for it. His life is synonymous with honest self-determination and freedom—the right to live his own way, under the law—as well as maintaining an abiding commitment to helping others. A cowboy is generous and open hearted, one who takes care of his own.

Cattlemen and cowboys are a special breed. They know you can't run a good ranch alone. It's teamwork that leads to a sense of community and brotherhood, and to be a cowboy is to be part of a team. After more than a century of raising cattle, this enduring steward of the land has attained iconic status, no longer represented by any one man, living or deceased, but by the job. For to live

Top: Inca Ware by Shenanago China, a remarkably detailed drawing of a cowboy herding a cow, red glaze decal on tan body, circa 1950s.
Above: Gail and Dan Allen chasing a stray on Broken Spear Ranch, La Junta, Colorado, 2008. (Courtesy Tim Erickson)

as a cowboy is to commit to a challenging way of life, in spite of all its risks, and accept that it's a good and rewarding life at that. Gender notwithstanding, that goes for cowgirls, too.

As is clearly indicated on the dinnerware I've collected, ones that reflect artistic interpretations and attitudes expressed over seventy long years, the cowboy has morphed from a specific individual drawn in great detail to a bold silhouetted figure with universal anonymity. Details like clothing and facial expressions have given way to the outline of a man of action, known from a distance by his broad shoulders and distinctive hat, ever astride his horse.

Yes, we know who he is. No explanations are needed. He's become a symbol for everything he's been and that so many others desire to be—courageous, considerate, straight, and fair. In the rodeo arena or the branding pen, pushing a cow or driving a truck, he lives his life with regard for those who've gone before and in full consideration of those who will follow, and for all the children of cowboys yet to come.

"Maybe the cowboy represents the last of the free men."

—Casey Tibbs

Kinds of Cowboys

Cowboy—a person who engages in cattle work on horseback.

Buckaroo—one who cowboys in the style of the American buckaroo, a Spanish influenced cowboy residing primarily in the Great Basin desert of Idaho, Oregon, California, Nevada, and Utah. An Americanized version of *vaquero*, Spanish for someone who works with cattle.

Big Outfit Cowboy or Buckaroo—works on a ranch that falls into the category of a big cow outfit.

Family Ranch Cowboy—works on a family-sized ranch, possibly sharing some of the haying or farming tasks.

Feedlot Cowboy—rides pens and checks cattle at a feedlot.

Lease Pasture Cowboy—works the spring, summer, and fall months on a huge grazing lease pasture (private, coop, or government-controlled).

Auction Market Cowboy—moves cattle behind the scenes at a livestock market sale barn.

Weekend Cowboy—enjoys owning a horse, riding, and helping the neighbors for fun, but has a steady job and a retirement package elsewhere to support this hobby.

Pro Rodeo Cowboy—considered a professional athlete and travels to rodeos to make a living.

Amateur Cowboy—competes on the weekends at local rodeos or horse competitions.

Professional Performance Horse Cowboy (Horseman)—trains and shows horses in a variety of different events such as cutting, reining, and roping.

—Courtesy of *Western Horseman* and Tim O'Byrne "Cowboys and Buckaroos"

Above: Shenango China "Western Round-Up" Ranch Ware, a salad plate showing a cowboy with chuck wagon and herd in the background. Sepia on white glaze, circa 1960s.
Left: Fording a creek in Kentucky. Cowboys shown, left to right: Ron Gregory, Larry Gregory, and Don Gregory. (Courtesy Hoot Jones)
Below left: Rare vintage salad size plate, clay body possibly by Homer Laughlin. Date unknown. Glaze is highly cracked. The image of cowboys and pack horse—a true Western scene.

Cowgirl Motif

Personally, I'm glad I grew up at a time when cowgirls like Dale Evans showed up in my life each and every week until I was nearly a teen. She was beautiful, kind, and rode a handsome horse named Buttermilk. I thought it was perfectly normal that women lived on ranches and were married to singing cowboys.

Was there ever a more fetching portrait of a professional cowgirl from the 1920s? Bonnie McCarroll was beautiful and talented, but died a tragic early death in the rodeo arena. (Courtesy National Cowgirl Museum, Fort Worth, Texas)

Millions of little girls all over America watched Dale Evans, too, and had dreams of horses long before anyone created *My Little Pony*. Today's youth have no such parallel, and certainly no well-known cowgirl as a role model. Just ask the average urban twelve year old who Charmayne James is (one of the country's champion barrel racers), and they'll look at you with a blank stare.

Today's ranch aside, girls aren't limited to the roles of rodeo queen or ranch mom when they grow up. Cowgirls of all ages can compete in far more than barrel racing in the competition arena, and they do. Just as able as

She's the real deal and sits tall in the saddle. Emily Allen rides with the best of them. Daughter of Gail and Millie Allen, Broken Spear Ranch, La Junta, Colorado. (Courtesy Linda Sharon)

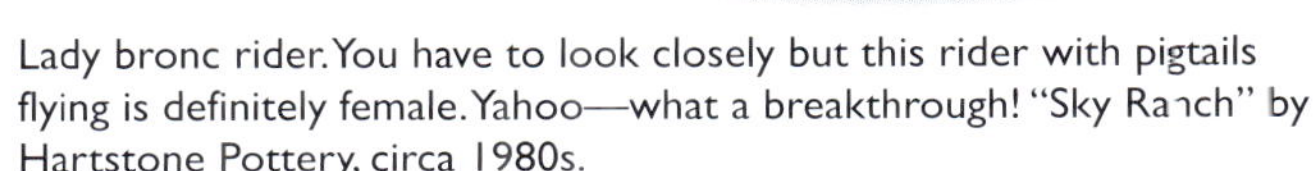

Lady bronc rider. You have to look closely but this rider with pigtails flying is definitely female. Yahoo—what a breakthrough! "Sky Ranch" by Hartstone Pottery, circa 1980s.

"If a man thinks that a woman who can dog steers, ride broncs, and ropes the wind is too much for him, he's probably right."

—Anonymous

Top: The 7L Ranch, Beaumont, Kansas. Action shot from left to right: Richell Bailey, Billie Franks, Rachel Lilley, Jodie Squier. (Courtesy Deb Fehlman Photography)
Above: Same team in action. These gals are worth any cowboy's respect, combining ranch skills, talent, and horsemanship. (Courtesy Deb Fehlman Photography)

Vintage-inspired images of cowgirls and bronc buster. "Vintage Ranch Collection" by Lynn Brown for Montana Lifestyles, circa 1990s.

men on horseback, and just as savvy about what's needed to run a ranch, most cowgirls start riding as soon as they can walk and take on whatever comes, growing up with the challenges of ranch life.

There's even a version of the Working Ranch Cowboys Association for women, and some of the toughest (and most feminine) gals I know compete in Weekend Ranch Rodeos, a demanding series of events that require superb horsemanship, roping skills, strength, and great reflexes.

Today's cowgirls are the mothers, daughters, sisters, and wives who keep the stock fed, the wheels turning, their families clothed, and the home fires burning on ranches all over the West. Many are educated in agricultural sciences and the cattle industry. They can round 'em up, rope and tie at a branding, help pull a calf, and cook up a storm when needed. For me, today's cowgirl is more of a heroine than ever.

> "Cowgirls can do everything a cowboy can do—they just look better doing it."
>
> —Anonymous

Hats off to the very few manufacturers who put a cowgirl on a dinner plate. It was about time. What better way to get the message to the people. Hartstone Pottery, Montana Lifestyles, and Pipestone are all manufacturers who have given cowgirls their due. Cowgirl UP!

CHAPTER 13

A Manufacturer's Guide to Dinnerware

Anyone embarking on a collection of Western dinnerware needs to know some basics to appreciate the various products circulating among dealers of vintage or contemporary restaurant ware.

One of the most reputable clearing houses in the country is Replacements Ltd., of North Carolina (www.replacements.com), a treasure trove of past and current patterns warehoused for the person who wants to replace or restore incomplete sets. Here, categories of china are neatly cross-referenced by subject matter, manufacturers, and pattern name. Replacement's assistance in this book has been invaluable, and as inventory and prices change, they remain a viable resource for checking values and availability. With their permission, the following guide is reprinted. It covers every type of dishware product one is likely to uncover in a lifetime of collecting.

A Brief History

Dinnerware pieces are among some of the first entirely man-made objects ever created, and nearly every primitive society produced dinnerware in some form. In

Grand Lodge dinnerware for Pendleton Home Collection, 100 percent vitrified china. Iconic tipi design taken straight from the company archives, and includes dinner and salad plate, soup and cereal bowl, plus serving pieces. (Courtesy Pendleton Company, Pendleton, Oregon)

"Wagon Wheel" pattern in prairie green glaze: a timeless example of the popular pottery made from local clays in Oklahoma by the Frankoma Pottery Company.

addition to their use as eating utensils, these early pieces were used for carrying water, cooking, and the storage of food.

The Chinese are credited with inventing what we know as dinnerware today, along with the development of processes over thousands of years that eventually led to the mixing of clay and stone to produce the first true porcelain ware. More developments led to the discovery of fireable clear and colored glazes, as well as individualized decoration. Chinese dinnerware pieces found their way to Europe via established trade routes with the west, where they became highly prized items. Formula and production processes used to produce dinnerware in England, France, and Germany were continually developed and refined, eventually yielding the fine patterns and dinnerware sets that we know today.

Today's dinnerware owes much of its development to advances made in clay bodies and glaze formulas, plus decorative methods and manufacturing techniques, which occurred in England's Staffordshire pottery district between 1750 and 1850. English designers and manufacturers set the dinnerware quality standards for the rest of the world, and are still the leaders in this field.

Ceramic dinnerware is produced in various categories using a mixture of raw materials, including different types and grades of clay, stone, glass, and bone ash. These materials, combined with standardized firing temperatures, produce dinnerware in different categories that include pottery and earthenware, stoneware, porcelain, and bone china.

Pottery is made from lower grade clay that is fired at relatively low temperatures, and does not become vitrified (hard and "glassy") or translucent after firing. For thousands of years, people have created pottery by molding pots, bowls, plates, and pitchers from clay and then baking them. Over the years pottery has come to be known by a number of names, including earthenware, semi-porcelain, graniteware, and ironstone. Unfinished pottery is typically somewhat porous with a thick, opaque, clay body. Pottery dinnerware patterns are made by companies like Pfaltzgraff, Mikasa, and thousands of others. Earthenware is similar to pottery, but it is usually more durable and suitable for everyday use.

Stoneware is very hard and dense. Stoneware dinnerware sets, in undecorated form, vary in color from brown to blue-gray. This type of clay is fired at very high temperatures and has a somewhat vitrified body that is water resistant and more durable than pottery. Several thousand stoneware dinnerware patterns are stocked at Replacements Ltd., as it's a very popular choice for restaurant and home use. Western-themed manufacturers include Montana Silversmiths and Triple Creek Products (Ironstone), to name only two.

Porcelain dinnerware is made from very high quality clay and is vitreous, nonporous, and in most cases

By Bing and Grondahl of Denmark, porcelain collector's plate, circa 1970s. (Plate courtesy Replacements, Ltd.)

Clever and practical deviled egg plate, one of dozens of sumptuous designs in bone china featuring vintage photography by Laton Huffman—durable and elegant. (Courtesy WesternWare Goods)

translucent. It is strong and light and thinner than many clay types. The commonly used generic term for dinnerware, "china," comes from the fact that porcelain was first made in China. It is believed that porcelain was first developed there during the ninth century. During the early 1700s, the process used to make porcelain found its way to the European continent. Two types of porcelain prevail: soft paste and hard paste. Soft paste porcelain combines white clay and ground glass, and it is fired at a lower temperature than hard paste porcelain, which is made from china, stone, and kaolin. A wide variety of porcelain dinnerware patterns are carried at Replacements, including many European manufacturers, such as Rosenthal, Lenox, and Haviland.

Bone china dinnerware includes the use of highly refined clay and bone ash in its production. Bone china came into being as a result of a number of experiments performed by English china manufacturers in the mid-eighteenth century. The English were seeking a process by which they could achieve "vitrification," in which the clay and feldspar bond during the firing, becoming one material. Unfortunately, the English were unable to get their kilns hot enough to achieve this fusion. Therefore, they sought to lower the required temperature at which vitrification would take place. By adding animal bone ash to the china compound, they were able to achieve the result at lower temperatures.

WesternWare oversized, footed 12-inch wide serving bowl showing four typical round-up scenes by Huffman. Front: two of four 5x7-inch hors d'oeuvres plates with cowboy images. Serving utensils by Vagabond House.

Josiah Spode was the first English producer to achieve success with this new process, and the result was a form of china that was both translucent and durable. Bone china offers advantages over porcelain, including being whiter in color, lighter in weight, and less brittle. A wider range of colors can also be used in its decoration. Well known manufacturers include Royal Albert, Wedgwood, and Chelsea. WesternWare of Montana uses bone china for its superb dinnerware.

CHAPTER 14

Collectors and Collecting

"Boots & Saddle"—still one of Wallace China's most popular designs, created originally by artist Till Goodan. Shown here, both vintage ware and current pieces made by True West Home. (Courtesy Janet Hix)

Janet Hix at home with a small part of her exceptional collection.

Collectors are a special breed. They collect because they have a passion, and nothing or no one in the world can stop them. I know people who collect Alfa Romeo cars and others who collect spurs, vintage photography, pin-up cuties, and Pez dispensers. I know a man who collects classic guitars and another who collects vintage gas pumps. It seems like wherever there's a collector, there's also an association or group of like-minded supporters, and often a magazine. Collecting becomes a subculture.

To me, collecting china is especially fascinating because it weds a craft to an art form and the art form to a culture. Since time began and primitive man fashioned his first vessel out of clay, we have traced our evolution through the clay arts. Cooking vessels are connected to food, and food is connected to region. Regions are about agriculture, which leads to harvest and seasonal festivals. Dishware made for serving food might just be the key to tracing man's passage through time and society's cultural change. After all, things made of clay reflect values, technology, sociology, matters of style, manners, and food preferences.

Along this journey I sought out many china collectors. My first were entrepreneurs Wil Garcia and Harvey Richards, former owners of Hooked on Glass in Denver, a veritable china and glass museum that, after twenty-five years, finally closed in 2009 due to the difficult times. Wil is a frequent docent at the Kirkland Museum in Denver, which has an enormous Mid-Century Modern china collection. He continues to guide others in their quest. But the most dedicated collector of Western china I've met to date is Janet Lewis Hix of Texas. In her own words, here is how it all began.

"I saw the reproduction pieces of Wallace at a local restaurant ten or twelve years ago. They caught my eye. Then, by accident, I chanced across a vintage piece of Wallace 'Westward Ho—Rodeo' ware on eBay. Always feeling that I had a cowgirl spirit, I was attracted to it. I decided to buy. After all, my great-great grandfather was a china and crystal importer and my mother was a collector. I grew up with a china and crystal collection."

Janet's passion for Wallace had begun. She mixed and matched lines and patterns at first in a hit-or-miss fashion, but as time went on she decided to collect full sets of patterns if she could. "For me," she explained, "the journey is the most fun—finding the pieces."

An avid on-line auction hunter, she's savvy about what and how to buy. In addition, she lives in the heart of what was once a rich retail area for Western china, so she peruses local auction and antique resources. She often shops local dealers, too, like the Montgomery

Complete set of "Westward Ho—Rodeo" pattern, illustrated by Till Goodan for Wallace China. Vintage and modern reproductions mixed. (Courtesy Janet Hix)

Street Antique Mall in Fort Worth, Texas. She once found a Till Goodan piece there that looked like tooled leather, a rare discovery. She also occasionally frequents a china business in Fort Worth called Dishes From the Past. Antique shows and local events like the NQHA (National Quarter Horse Association) Futurity are good opportunities, too.

"I get the feeling that most of what is found here locally was once purchased as souvenir items on trips to more westerly locales, since much of it was made by California manufacturers," Janet said.

Hix has attained a certain amount of celebrity for her passion and was written up by a local newspaper, the *Colleyville Courier,* which serves a tri-metro area. Although not a ranch-raised cowgirl, she has a profound love of Western culture and began her hobby in earnest in 1999. She chose Western china because the patterns were fun, informal, and a part of history. In addition, she has select glassware items, linens, and a myriad of complementary accessories from the 1930s through the '60s. She has a great eye for what's worth buying.

Today, Hix's collection is the envy of many. This year marks the fifth that she's entered the Texas State Fair, an event in which she's taken top honors five years in a row for her beautiful assembly of choice items, always different. Each entry must be comprised of three pieces and must be at least thirty years old.

"Every year grows more challenging," said Janet. She does worry that the judges may simply tire of selecting her, even if they feel the presentation is outstanding.

Kept in pristine condition, the enormous collection of over six-hundred pieces fills her home. She admits she doesn't have an accurate inventory. On occasion, she sells a piece or adds another. "In the early days of collecting I wouldn't take a piece that had a chip on it," she said, "and let some rare items get away. Now I know better."

Hix's collection includes almost all the Wallace patterns, plus a unique collection of salt and pepper shakers, and Wallace ashtrays portraying Western personalities like Will James, Kit Carson, and Buffalo Bill Cody. She has only one piece of the seldom-circulated "Old West 49er" pattern, a rare find in any area.

Upper left: Will Rogers collection by Wallace China.
Lower left: Ash trays dedicated to Western heroes and historical figures.
Right: Western-themed salt and pepper shakers by Wallace, Vernon Kilns, and others. (Courtesy Janet Hix)

Above: Again, one of the many remarkable complete collections of Wallace China owned by Janet Hix. "Westward Ho—Longhorn" collection by Till Goodan. What a beautiful table. (Courtesy Janet Hix)
Right: Broken dinnerware brands from Wallace China—so effective as wall décor in Janet's kitchen on a tiled wall. Three letters spell HIX, of course. (Courtesy Janet Hix)

Janet displays her collection with pride and authority, having become increasingly knowledgeable about her cache. Her home is a showcase, with most of the pieces in her kitchen and family room. Plates adorn the empty space above the cabinets, other items are framed and hang on the wall. Bowls are nestled and stacked to save space.

"I read somewhere," she said, "that if your china/crystal/silver is too good for your family and friends, then it's too good to own. So I use my china on special occasions."

This collector adds her *joie de vivre* to all she does. The china collection is just an extension of her wider appreciation of the West, its literature and its art, and her love of home, friends, and family. Her interest and assistance in this project has been invaluable and the addition of her beautifully styled photos has enriched this book. Nowhere else could I imagine finding such impressive and complete collections. It's heartwarming to see the many accessory pieces shown together with the full place settings, and it's been a rare privilege to peek inside her home and enjoy what she has so carefully cultivated.

A collector like Janet reminds us that we can all become stewards of a fading past. Col-

In *Collecting the Old West* by Jim and Nancy Schaut, the authors propose that things Western speak to the collector in us all. Many Americans and citizens of other countries consider themselves Western enthusiasts. "It's not necessary to go west of the Mississippi to find prime Western memorabilia. I have heard time and time again from dealers and collectors that the best Western memorabilia can be found in the Far East or Japan. Souvenirs that were purchased on excursions to the West were taken home and stored for years. When they do surface, they're generally in exquisite condition. Cowboy kitsch in particular has grabbed the imagination of decorators and collectors alike and has great potential."

lecting is preservation. Hopefully, some day a worthy repository, a museum perhaps, will make hers available for all the world to see.

"Pioneer Trails" and "El Rancho" by Wallace China—both collections are splendid in their entirety. Absolute works of art, displayed in many pieces. (Courtesy Janet Hix)

Finding Vintage Western Dinnerware

Locating collectible dinnerware is often a mixture of luck and chance. It pays to befriend an antique or Western collectibles dealer and let them know what you're looking for. Estate sales, auction houses, and flea markets are good places to look, especially if you enjoy the thrill of the hunt and have plenty of time.

Craig's List and eBay are excellent resources on the Internet. For basic education and history about commercial products, you can also go to Restaurantwarecollectors.com. There you'll find valuable information, fascinating lore regarding manufacturers, back stamps, history, chat boards, and more—a great way to learn about the identification process. Take note of back stamps. They are the identification and dating system for all china and porcelain, and they change over time. Guides on various producers are accessible in reference books and are well worth reading.

Assorted back stamps can tell you much about the history of a piece. Guides to the back stamp are available in many reference books and are a fun way to authenticate and date your collection.

New products by modern vendors can be found at many Western lifestyle boutiques and larger Western retail stores across the country. Catalogs and online sites carry them, as well. Happy hunting.

CHAPTER 15

Collector Plates

You might ask why collector plates would be found in a book on dinnerware. After all, you can't use them for food consumption or serve on them. But they are deeply linked to Western history, personalities, and legends. Strictly decorative, I like to think of them as the mass-market substitute for fine art—something like an everyman's wall décor.

The history of collector plates commemorating a place, person, or historical event goes back to eighteenth-century England. The French, Italians, Germans, and Danes all made them, too. As the art form of fine china production grew, so did the complexity and importance of these historical markers.

This beautiful state plate with its detailed black and white depiction of pioneers in their covered wagons is a treasure. The passage of a century is depicted around its rim showing the buffalo, the Indians, the pioneer, the rancher, the farmer, the trains that crossed the West and finally, the airplane. It was made in England by Wedgwood for the Crosby Brothers of Topeka, Kansas. I am guessing it was made around 1961, since the State of Kansas celebrated its centennial then.

The plate bears the following explanation on the back: "Coronado was the first white man to see these rolling plains, grazing places of the buffalo. In time, the buffalo gave way to the wagon trains on the old Santa Fe and Oregon Trails and thousands more white men came to start a new life in the West. The early homesteaders first built sod houses. Tremendous cattle drives came up from Texas to the railheads of Abilene, Wichita, and Dodge City. Now these plains are vast wheat farms and the towering elevators and modern industry are monuments to the first hundred years and a challenge to future generations."

Imported plate made in Czechoslovakia, circa 1950.

enduring subjects like wildlife and birds are popular at the moment. But in the past, the range of subjects was diverse: the public has loved fairy tales, historical figures, war heroes, film stars, royalty, politicians, and even cartoon characters.

Despite the fact that collector plates were made in multiples, they were produced in limited editions. Almost all were made of porcelain, a highly vitreous type of clay body that's lighter than ironstone or pottery and more translucent. It takes color very well.

Most plates came with certificates authenticating the production (and still do), stating the name of the artist, the manufacturer, when the plate was made, and why. Some manufacturers used better technology than others, hence their color reproductions were clearer and

I remember seeing ads in Sunday newspaper magazines during the 1970s and '80s offering a new edition plate by a U.S. plate maker commemorating a holiday, an event, a film star, a famous artist, or the latest hero. I recall plates decorated with howling wolves, eagles, and Native Americans. Although no one I knew collected them, I'm sure that someone had to. They are heavily traded and collected today.

Like many other temporal means of recording events and subjects, their popularity is short lived. More

John Wayne: One of the many versions of the famed actor depicted on a collector plate. I especially like this one and its down to earth portrayal of him as a cowboy wearing chaps, carrying a Winchester, and hauling a saddle. Titled "Spirit of the West," the original image was painted by Robert Tanenbaum. The plate is porcelain and trimmed in 24-carat gold, by Franklin Mint.

more saturated. Just a few of the legendary European producers were Bing & Grondahl, Royal Copenhagen, Royal Doulton, and Wedgwood. Of past and current note in the U.S. are the Danbury Mint, Franklin Mint, and Bradford Exchange.

As a popular decorative gift item, the heyday for production of collector plates was the 1970s and '80s. It seemed like anyone with a china factory was in the business. Eventually the market was flooded, and one by one companies started to bail out. Many of the European factories persisted. Bing & Grondahl, a key survivor, has actually been producing commemorative giftware since 1895, and since 1908 so has Royal Copenhagen.

Frederic Remington sold a reproduction license to the Gorham company, one of the top twenty manufacturers of quality china here in the United States. Gorham singled out specific characters, a marvelous rogue's gallery of mountain men, Indians, and cowboys originally painted by Remington as singular works of art. The reproductions were extremely well made and have become more collectable of late. The Franciscan China Company also made dinnerware and collector plates utilizing works by Remington. He proved a hugely popular artist.

It's worth noting that a vast difference in finished works can be expected from any one company. The evolution of color reproduction methods accounts for noticeable differences in accuracy, depth of color, and clarity. The most significant changes however, have occurred since 1970.

Buffalo Bill Cody's Farewell (5th edition) and Royal Visit (8th Edition), by Copenhagen Porcelain–Bing and Grondahl, 14 carat gold trim. Both plates commemorate the 100th Anniversary of Buffalo Bill's Wild West from the original paintings by Jack Woodson. Authorized by the United States Historical Society and the Buffalo Bill Historical Center. Limited edition of 5,000.

Robert Goins, collectible plate specialist at Replacements Ltd., believes the older ware was actually better. "Back in the 1970s," he explained, "you basically had to recreate the art and then color-separate it. Technology has changed so much. Today you're using a desktop computer and regenerating the image. The colors are separated and laid down much like a color print or giclée, except that instead of inks the colors are actually liquid glaze. When fired, they fuse and the colors become brilliant and true, creating a reproduction of the original photo or work of art. Various levels of this technology can be found, pending what one is willing to pay for."

"Catch Me If You Can" by Royal Cornwall Ltd., 1982, from the series entitled "Memories of the Western Prairies," a limited edition. Original painting is by Rosemary Calder.

Wittnauer Collector's Guild, American Masterpiece Collection, fine bone china made in England. Original painting can be found at the Amon Carter Museum of Western Art in Fort Worth, Texas. Frederic Remington produced more than 2,700 paintings and drawings in his lifetime. "A Dash for Timber" is considered one of his most forceful works and at auction brought the largest sum ever paid for one of his paintings.

The American West has long been a favored subject, especially its Indians and wild creatures. The few samples highlighted in this chapter reveal the depth of interest in telling our Western story. From the dignity of Buffalo Bill appearing before the Queen of England, to the enchanting scene of a pioneer girl playing a game of chase on her horse, collectible china manufacturers embraced a myriad of subjects.

The elegant Wittnauer reproduction of the Remington painting is an exceptional example exquisitely framed in its gilded rim. And if the almost iridescent plates from the series honoring the television Westerns leave you curious—you're not the only one. Dale and Roy and Tonto and the Lone Ranger all have a strange reality about them, as if created in super-Technicolor.

"That's because," explained Goins, "the original photos that these were made from were taken in black and white. These photos were colored, after the fact."

I say, cringe and bear it. I found them irresistible anyway. They may not be dinnerware, but they're certainly collectible.

Happy Trails to You

Top: "Lone Ranger and Tonto" from the Classic TV Westerns Plate Collection, a limited edition series of fine porcelain plates presented by the Hamilton Collection by Palladium Media Enterprises in 1990 (plate #4181 A). Left "Dale Evans and Roy Rogers" also from the Classic TV Westerns Plate Collection, a limited edition series by the "Hamilton" collection and Roy. Rogers Enterprises, Inc. (plate #099sc). The above two plates, part of the author's collection, are completed in the series by "Bonanza," "Hopalong Cassidy" on his horse Topper, "Rawhide," "Have Gun Will Travel," and "The Virginian."

CHAPTER 16

Dinnerware Manufacturing Today

A Day in the Life of a Dinner Plate

At a time when the term "Made in America" has become a rarity, most American consumers appreciate any company that still can make the claim. There's something sacred about keeping the production of any tangible, useful product between our shores when market conditions indicate that it's probably easier, cheaper, and faster to make it overseas.

Therefore, it's important to acknowledge those few china manufacturers in the U.S. still committed to the process. One of these, H.F. Coors in Tucson, Arizona, is still manufacturing tableware in the time-honored tradition—on site and step-by-step, through carefully monitored semi-mass-production methods, with hand finishing, hand decorating, and inspection. In fact, they're making the Wallace Western china reproduction, a process that's worth seeing.

Dirck Schou, the dedicated owner of H.F. Coors, Tuscon, Arizona, an all-American dinnerware factory.

True West Home dinnerware pieces. Items are available for immediate sale or special ordered on site.

Dirck Schou, majority owner and CEO of H.F. Coors, can be proud of the sixty-person team he oversees in his factory on the desert's edge. Here, mass-produced goods like mugs and dinnerware sets are turned out, as well as stunning hand-painted custom stoneware items created by staff artist Bob DeArmond. Custom tableware is created on a to-order basis for a number of well-known clients and distributors, such as the famous basket company, Longaberger; the upscale Michael Wainwright Company of Massachusetts; and True West Home (makers of the original Wallace Western dinnerware) of Royse City, Texas.

Schou, an engineer and MBA by training, learned the ceramic manufacturing trade by working for Pfaltzgraff in York, Pennsylvania, and through his ownership of Simpsons Potters Ltd. of Stoke-on-Trent, Staffordshire, England—companies with well-earned reputations for quality china. He returned to America and began his own operation in his hometown of Tucson in 1990, when he and his partner David Sounart formed Catalina China. In 2003, they saved H.F. Coors from oblivion when they purchased it from a conglomerate that was closing it down for its real estate value. They acquired state-of-the art mixers, grinders, forming machines, mold-making materials, plus a massive kiln, enabling them to convert Catalina into a full-scale china operation. Now they had everything necessary to handle the basic chemistry of clay mixing, all the way through to perfectly finished, glazed, and hand-decorated individual pieces.

Schou loves the process. From the many powdery bags of minerals and silica, he oversees the mixing of materials in huge vats and the subsequent purification of the resulting product. The mixture, once fluid, passes

Bob DeArmand is in-house designer shown with samples of his brilliant dinnerware designs.

Greenware—just one of the many stages of production.

through a sieve to remove any impurities. (The clay itself and necessary elements come from as far away as Kentucky, Tennessee, Georgia, and Illinois, direct from the clay mines.)

The liquid clay is made into molded cakes by removing 80 percent of the water in massive filter presses. That product is then chopped up, run through a vacuum chamber, and reconstituted in a pug mill, creating the actual malleable clay wads, or pugs, which will later be pressed into shapes in the plaster of Paris molds.

Master molds are made by casting models of items that are handmade of plaster by a highly skilled modeler. The model is then encased in a block where a full impression is created. Once the model is removed from the block, the two halves of the mold hold within them the "negative." This block-mold allows for the creation of a case mold out of which liquid plaster is used to cast multiple production molds. Each production mold runs through a jigger, a unique machine that presses and spins the clay into the product shape. Once the new shapes are released as a result of heating and drying, they're hand-trimmed and smoothed to perfection.

It's interesting to note that a typical clay product shrinks 12 percent from its first forming in clay to its

The mold library—it's important to keep the original mold of every single design.

final fired shape, and since every piece is affected by humidity, all items go through an automatic drying process as precaution against cracking.

A mold can be used to make up to one hundred pieces with accuracy. Master molds are kept in a "library" of sorts, since creating them is time-consuming, and they're a valuable record as well as a necessary starting point. They represent the ability to reproduce any design made in the past if there's a call for it. Some items are produced by additional shaping via a special press. In one instance, in the making of a particular platter, it is subjected to 120 tons of pressure that neatly forms the platter to the exact curve and density desired.

Pre-manufactured glazes are not used here—glazes are actually mixed on the premises from brightly colored calcined minerals and applied to products that have been unmolded and dried. By making their own glazes, H.F. Coors can control the flow and purity, assuring that the glaze won't drip, run, craze, or crawl. The glazes used here are opaque, some matt and some shiny, giving all the pieces a lustrous opaque color, be it off-white or a specific hue. Some products receive delicate airbrushing over the glaze, or even gilding with liquid gold glaze.

Finally, all the glazed ware is loaded onto platforms or kiln cars that move slowly on a conveyor belt through the massive kiln that fires them to a temperature of 2,320 degrees F. A staggering total of 15,000 pieces can be fired in one day.

Some items are plain, and others are decorated, like the "Westward Ho—Rodeo" collection, with its center decals and brands around the edge. Patient workers hand-apply decal images (created by decal companies in California or back East) that are received on clear transfer sheets. Once in the kiln, the backing sheet material, or cover coat, burns away from the decals, allowing the layers of color—composed of glaze elements themselves—to fuse into the glaze on the clay body. (Other products are carefully hand decorated by several resident hand painters.) Only through this process can products be suitable enough for restaurant use.

Although highly simplified, this walk-through is intended to reveal a mere hint of the complexity and control needed to turn out perfect dinnerware. The humble dinner plate is actually the end result of a carefully orchestrated series of steps. Without understanding that, no collector can appreciate the value of the ware.

It's remarkable how a design can be translated into a transferable sheet of glaze on tissue that, once heated, becomes glass-like and fuses onto the clay.

CHAPTER 17

Manufacturers by the Decade

Thirty years isn't very long for a collectible to be established, but essentially the years from 1940 through 1970 mark the beginning and end of the vintage collectible Western china era. A look at the decades following World War II shows how the trends in entertainment encouraged various aspects of Western popular culture. Literature, film, and celebrities have always helped drive the visibility of all things Western. It helps to see these many manufacturers' goods against a tableau of events and ideas.

The 1940s

The shadow of World War II and the Nazi Holocaust darkened everything during the first half of this decade. Its end in 1945 meant a long period of recovery, at home and abroad. America welcomed soldiers returning home, factories starting up again, and a renewed sense of nationalism and patriotism celebrating a victor's role in the world.

This was the era of the atomic age simmering beneath Cold War politics that would last for the next twenty years. The United Nations

Hopalong Cassidy plate from 1949–'50, produced by W.S. George Fine Dinnerware. Founded in 1904 in East Palestine, Ohio, by William Shaw George, the company made semi-porcelain dinnerware as well as hotel and bath products. They expanded and prospered for over sixty years, finally closing in 1974. They made all of Hopalong Cassidy's licensed dinnerware and children's sets. Matching cup and bowl shown on page 37.

was formed. Harry S. Truman took over from Franklin Roosevelt with a firm hand. Meanwhile, jet propulsion, nuclear power, and a renewed commitment to production would follow. But with the end of food rationing and people going back to work, a new type of middle class arose, followed by a baby boom and the growth of cities and urban expansion.

Entertainment was at its peak, the only refuge during the war years. Hollywood made some of its most classic films, with actors like Humphrey Bogart and Jimmy Stewart, and famed directors like Orson Wells and Frank Capra. Disney created *Fantasia* and *Bambi,* and comedian Bob Hope and singer Bing Crosby entertained a nation.

Western movies, already firmly in place in the 1930s, grew in popularity. By the '40s, subgenres of Westerns began to evolve in an attempt to cater to different audiences. Traditional Westerns made then, like *Northwest Passage, Billy the Kid* and *The Westerner,* served one market; *Go West* with the Marx brothers served another, introducing the Comedy Western. *They Died with Their Boots On* and *She Wore A Yellow Ribbon* brought us the Cavalry Western. In the 1940s, the *King of the Cowboys* with Roy Rogers gave us the Singing Western, and *Duel in the Sand,* the first Sex Western. Humphrey Bogart starred in one of the first Psychological Westerns, *The Treasure of the Sierra Madre.* The '40s also showcased the first serials for children, like *The Lone Ranger* and *The Adventures of Cylcone Malone. Howdy Doody,* with the smiling puppet by the same name, and his puppeteer, Buffalo Bob, debuted in 1947.

The elaborate fashions of the singing cowboys inspired all manner of casual wear for the mass market, and the Western clothing industry as a fashion statement was born. Nudie suits (sequined, embroidered, and personalized Western wear, made by Los Angles designer Nudie Cohen) began to adorn the stars, and fringed shirts became all the rage. With the works of Zane Grey and Louis L'Amour on the bookshelves, the Western defined mass entertainment in a way never seen before. The first inklings that Western images would soon follow on everything from furniture to dinnerware had surfaced.

Holman China
1947–1970

This short history of a little-known china manufacturer serves perfectly to illustrate the various elements that shaped America's dinnerware business at the end of the 1940s. These include returning soldiers, a search for work leading to creative entrepreneurship, and the barbecue craze—a novelty that took America by storm.

The name "Holman Company" first appeared on the back of an unusual china plate I found early in my collecting. That name and the words "Frisco" were the only hints of where to begin to look for background information. Holman isn't mentioned anywhere in the many archives of American pottery manufacturers that I own. But the dinnerware intrigued me, and I was determined to learn more about it and find other examples.

That first small bread and butter plate with brands around the rim and a cactus in the middle seemed part of a larger puzzle. I knew there had to be a set. Several months later, when six of the dinner plates showed up with an eBay seller, I bought them all. But I was still no farther ahead.

I decided to look into Frisco, Texas, myself, and do some prowling around on the Internet. My search for more background on this company led me to the town's historical society and Robert Warren, a former mayor (retired) and president of the society. He in turn referred me to a marvelous resource in Dallas, Texas, Elizabeth Pink, a woman who grew up in the small Texas town of Frisco, herself.

She remembered when the Holman factory was actually in business and, over a wonderful phone call, revealed all the rest. Here is her account:

Left: Once in a while, dinnerware artwork features a cactus. This one holds its own as an image of the West. Holman China, Frisco, Texas, circa 1940s.

Above: This bucking bronco plate by Holman China with large readable brands around the rim makes a wonderfully cohesive design—a stunning table service in its day.

"The Holman Company was made up of three friends who served in World War II together: Earl Standerfer, a Frisco boy; R.K. Hollas [from Fredericksberg, Texas] and Robert Menefee [origin unknown]. Hollas and Menefee formed the Holman Company in about 1947 and had an office and a workplace on the main street in Frisco. It was a building about 40 feet wide by 120 feet in length, full of long tables with silk-screening materials. They employed ten to twelve people making chef's hats, barbecue aprons, and T-shirts [the artist/designer was Menefee). The plates apparently came manufactured, ready for a decal and final glazing, and the brand design on the lip of the plate matched the barbecue aprons. The boxed sets included a mug, dinner and salad plates, and a deep cereal bowl.

"The pottery manufacture was apparently a short term thing, perhaps only ten years. The company ceased production altogether in 1970. Mr. Menefee moved to Dallas, and Hollas moved to Mineral Wells, Texas." (Footnote: all parties appear to be deceased.)

A short history of Frisco, Texas
In 1843, at Bird's Fort in Tarrant County, Texas, the treaty between the Indians and the "whites" was signed. This made north Texas technically safe for Anglo-American home seekers. Sometime before 1858, a settlement was started with the arrival of prairie schooners, and that settlement eventually became Lebanon, Texas. In 1902, the Frisco railroad was completed and the better part of Lebanon moved houses and stores to the site of the railroad, three miles northwest. Frisco is located in West Collin County and was incorporated in 1908. The population in 1930 was 618. It grew to 842 by 1954, and now in 2009, boasts 110,000.

—Elizabeth Pink

Wallace China
1931–1964

Wallace China was founded in Vernon, California, in 1931, and began as a commercial manufacturer of heavy gauge commercial china, mostly sold for institutional purposes. Founded originally by Wallace B. Wood, the sprawling factory in Huntington Park, near Los Angeles, produced vitreous china in a white or tan base color under a variety of trademarks, such as "Desert Ware," "Pueblo Ware," and of course, the almost legendary collection known as "Westward Ho."

"Westward Ho—Rodeo" by Wallace China—all the various pieces and serving ware, so full of life. (Courtesy True West Home)

A series of varying back stamps chronicles the history of Wallace for some thirty years with a wide variety of identification marks.

In the 1930s, American retail dinnerware for home use was still dominated by many traditional English

These fun little cartoon cowboys and their small herd were a novel idea. The artist is unknown. The plate came in 3 sizes: this one is 8-1/4 inches and very heavy. It's actually marked "Shenango of California," which means it was made between 1959 and 1964 after Wallace China was bought by Shenango China.

Wallace China from the 1940s and '50s: "Chuck Wagon" pattern, found in two color combinations, a tan body or a white body with rust transfer, generally unmarked on the back. Distributor of the pattern was the El Paso Hotel Supply, El Paso, Texas. Water pitcher is vintage Fiesta Ware by Homer Laughlin.

designs reflecting popular taste. Among other patterns, Wallace actually produced the well-known and widely collected "Willow" pattern (transferware) in several monochromatic colors. An early Wallace Western restaurant ware collection, circa the late 1940s, was the ware made for the El Paso Hotel called "Round Up," showing a chuck wagon cookout scene on a tan clay body.

Another collection was based on the Gold Rush and called "The '49ers." But it wasn't until 1943, when the M.C. Wentz Company of southern California approached the Wallace Company, that they first created a line of informal china, referred to by Wentz as "barbecue ware," with a Western theme suitable for casual dining as well as institutional use.

Wentz hired Los Angeles artist Till Goodan to create the decorations, and four patterns resulted, as well as a special children's set called "Little Buckaroo," all on a tan clay body with dark and light brown imagery. The "Rodeo" pattern was accented by additional colors that were hand-painted under the glaze. Later on, some of "Westward Ho" was also released in mission blue or brown on a white background.

Following the line's immediate success, another pattern was debuted by Wallace China dubbed "El Rancho" (artist unknown). As shown earlier in this book, this group was decorated with evocative Western landscapes and town scenes, designs that seemed perfect for the era and the many Western films that provided similar imagery.

Soon after came the stunning set created by Goodan known as "Pioneer Trails," with a series of images depicting the way West, with stagecoaches, Indians in head-

Early Wallace China, circa1950s, "The 49ers" pattern devoted to the Gold Rush with detailed scenes of miner's life. Top photo courtesy of collector Lane Wintermute; bottom photo with goldpanner from author's collection. Oval under platter by Cowboy Living, "Barbwire" Collection.

"Pioneer Trails" by Wallace China, circa 1950s. The depiction of the stage coach and freight hauling teams are worthy of a Western museum. Original artwork by Till Goodan. (Courtesy Janet Hix)

dresses on their horses, and the pioneer in his prairie schooner led by oxen. The power of the original art and the success of the transfer to stoneware makes these plates exceptional. The border design is a caravan of horses and wagons—a beautiful flow of line and form in sepia glaze.

In 1959, Wallace China was taken over by the Shenango China Company of Newcastle, Pennsylvania, who continued to serve Wallace's customers for a few more years. A 1961 sales brochure shows twenty-four separate items still for sale at that time, but shortly thereafter the factory succumbed to the changing market conditions. It was finally closed down in 1964.

"Westward Ho"— The Start of a Trend

"Westward Ho" was in many ways the true starting point for the many manufacturers of Western-themed dinnerware to follow. As once said by Tyler Beard, author and collector of Western vintage memorabilia and the first person to reintroduce Wallace's Western patterns, "Wallace China's 'Westward Ho' collection was the gold standard—the Cadillac of product." In terms of good design, durability, and charm, as well as the number of pieces still in use and in circulation today, one can hardly argue.

Artist Till Goodan left a considerable mark on the history of this beloved line, now widely collected and selling for somewhat daunting prices. Born in Eaton,

Self portrait, Till Goodan shown on horseback, a cowboy and a gentleman. (Courtesy True West Home)

Colorado, he moved to California in 1905. He rode horses in his youth, eventually hiring on with the famed Miller and Lux Ranch in California. There, he packed mules and ran pack trains into the High Sierras. He also broke horses and found time to enter local rodeos, riding saddle broncs, a tough sport for any cowboy. According to his biography in a 1945 *China and Glass* magazine article, he competed successfully until a horse actually went through a fence with him and put a hold on his rodeo career.

"Pioneer Trails" by Wallace China. Each and every plate and platter told a story. Indians on the lookout on left, gold panner on right, pioneer center.

All along, Goodan would draw and sketch images of ranch life and rodeo scenes, perfecting a style that would later become his trademark. By 1917, he turned to his interest in art full time, and studied with some of the best in the business in the California area. As he grew more prolific, he tried oil painting, watercolor, and lithographs. He later assumed a position as art director for the Richfield Oil Company, but finally left again to devote himself full time to his art. In time, he was discovered by the W.C. Wentz Company, a giftware producer and distributor that commissioned him to create a full line of accessories in ceramic, bronze, leather, paper, and fabric. The most famous of his signature lines, however, was the "Westward Ho" dinnerware produced by Wallace China for Wentz, in four distinctly different themes: "Pioneer Trails," "Longhorn," "Boots & Saddle," and "Rodeo."

"Boots & Saddle": Photo courtesy True West Home; image property of New West Creation.

The various patterns show lifelike scenes of broncos, steer wrestlers, pioneers, Indians, Western gear, and more, hand-applied in transfer decals, one color at a time. Longhorn cattle and cowboys circle the cups and plates in the "Longhorn" series; bold cattle brands in dark brown surround the "Westward Ho" pieces.

For the "Rodeo" collection, Goodan actually created a brand codex that accompanied the dinnerware sets—a complete guide to all the brands that embellished the pieces. Amid the many brands depicted were the famed

Flying A brand of Gene Autry's ranch; the brand of the 101, the famous Wild West show outfit with headquarters in Oklahoma; the O Bar O brand of a New Mexico ranch where Billy the Kid once hid out; the J-Four brand of Will Rogers' father; and the Pitchfork brand from one of the legendary ranches of Texas, among others—a total of 122 different brands in all. Studying the brand book is like reading a condensed version of the history of the West.

"Westward Ho," especially the "Rodeo" pattern, became hugely successful and was acquired by hotels, cafes, restaurants, and ranches. Celebrities of the day, like Gene Autry and Bing Crosby, owned sets as well. According to Cheryl Rogers Barnett, a daughter of Roy Rogers and Dale Evans, her parents actually received a set as a wedding present from the president of Republic Pictures. Not surprisingly, the pattern was so popular it was also widely imitated.

The Rules Book

Till Goodan was commissioned to be the illustrator for the original Rodeo Association of America's *Rodeo Contest Rules Book,* first published in 1942. This small pamphlet was a jewel of a publication with full-page illustrations. Several of these action-packed renditions of rodeo cowboys and rough stock were adapted for the "Westward Ho—Rodeo" pattern, and have proven to be timeless.

According to a 1945 *China and Glass* magazine, Goodan's artwork was without reproach. "Till Goodan is one of the few American artists who can draw a bucking horse to suit the critical taste of a bronc rider. The reason is simple. Till Goodan draws what he knows."

Goodan established a permanent home in Hollywood, as well as a ranch near the town of Lebec, and a mountain retreat in the Sierras. He started a family and bequeathed his passion for ranch life, horses, and art to his beloved daughter, Betty (Andrews) Goodan, who became a committed horsewoman in her own right and a champion cowgirl.

Betty was also a talented artist and illustrated the Roy Rogers paint books that were released in 1944 and 1946. Earlier, her father had illustrated the Gene Autry comic books that were first published in 1942 by Fawcett publishing. These are the most collectible because they contain Goodan's artwork. In the 1950s, Dell Publishing continued the series with the work of other artists.

The Golden Age of Illustration

Till Goodan was fortunate to come to light as an artist and illustrator during a time when illustration in America was at its peak. From the 1930s through the '50s, most magazines employed illustrators for both cover art and story illumination. This period was referred to by many as a golden age of illustration, thanks to huge advances in color printing technology. Illustrators left their mark on war posters, film poster art, fashion advertising, and in magazines like *Colliers, Redbook,* and the *Saturday Evening Post.* Realist artists like Norman Rockwell characterized the era.

Western pulp magazines, Western paperback novels, and comic books had brought Western stories to a nation for decades. They were illustrated by great artists like Tom Lovell, Warren Baumgartner, and Everett Raymond Kinstler, to name just a few. By the 1950s, the American public had developed a keen eye and an appreciation for the narrative artist and the West as portrayed through various print media, until the novelty of television destroyed the market. The dinnerware artist created for a consumer who could savor good Western illustration.

The cover and illustrations shown are some of the same that appear on the "Rodeo" pattern in the Wallace "Westward Ho" collection. (With thanks to Betty Goodan Andrews)

Riders and horses for each day will be selected by management: horses to be furnished by management and riders will draw for mounts. If rider draws a horse he has once ridden during this contest, he must draw again. Contestants must ride as often, and on any horse, as judges deem necessary to determine winner. Riding to be done with plain halter. ONE rein and saddle, all of which will be furnished by the management. Saddles to be recognized and accepted association 14½ to 15-inch tree made and rigged on the Hambley design. When new saddles are bought they shall be 15-inch tree. Rein to be three or four strand braided grass or cotton rope and not to exceed one inch in diameter, without tape and knots and must not be wrapped around hand. One arm free. Riders must not change hands on rein and rein hand must show daylight above horse's neck as riders leave chute. Riding rein and hand must be on same side. Horses to be saddled in chute or arena as management may direct. Rider

may cinch own saddle or examine same to determine if satisfactory. The matter of re-rides will be decided by the judges. After the horse leaves the starting place, everything the rider does will be counted for or against him. Horse must be spurred first jump out of starting place and rider must continue to spur throughout ride to satisfaction of judges. Where three judges are used, one judge to mark horse and two judges to mark the ride, the three figures only to be added to determine the total points.

Bucking horse contest to be timed at all member

Any of the following offenses will disqualify a rider:

Cheating in any manner;
Being bucked off;
Changing hands on reins;
Wrapping rein around hand;
Pulling leather;
Losing stirrup;
Not being ready to ride when called;
Failing to spur throughout ride to the satisfaction of judges;
Use of any substance or preparation on any part of rider's clothing or on any part of his equipment; riding otherwise than with straight rein from halter ring to rider; riding with locked rowels, or rowels that will lock on spurs. (The judges will examine clothing, saddle, rein, and spurs and exception will be made if local rules make necessary the covering of spur rowels.)

2

Steer Wrestling

14

Arena conditions will determine start and deadline rules; penalties for violations of these rules are matters for local determination. Wrestler must catch steer from horse.

There shall be three timers, a deadline referee, a field judge, and as many other officials as the local management finds necessary. Animals used for this contest should be closely inspected and objectionable ones eliminated. Contestant will be disqualified if he attempts to, in any way, tamper with steers or chutes. Only one hazer allowed. Contestant must furnish own hazers and horses. After catching steer, wrestler must bring it to a stop and twist it down. If steer is accidentally knocked down or thrown down before being brought to a stop, or is thrown by wrestler putting animal's horns into ground, it must be let up on all four feet and then thrown. Steer will be considered down only when it is lying flat on its side, all four feet out and head straight. The fairness of catch and throw will be left to the judges and their decision will be final.

Hazer must retire from field as soon as wrestler catches his steer and must not render any assistance to contestant while contestant is working with steer. Failure to observe this rule will impose penalty on contestant.

There will be a time limit of two minutes in this contest. If wrestler has not caught and thrown his steer in two minutes, he will retire from arena on signal and be given no time.

Ten seconds penalty for beating or breaking barrier.

No penalty for breaking horn.

15

As a painter in the realistic tradition, Goodan depicted not only the California landscape, but also the Arizona and New Mexico desert. His paintings can be found in collections throughout the West. A true Westerner who loved the lifestyle, he sadly suffered a heart attack in May of 1958 while astride his horse, serving as Grand Marshall for the Tulare, California, rodeo.

Daughter Betty still resides in the Los Angeles area and looks after the protection of Till Goodan's name and the rights to his work. In a series of interviews, it wasn't surprising to find out that vivid and fond memories of her father still sustain her and her children. In her own words:

"Collector Janet Hix in Texas has a wonderful collection of Goodan artwork, as do three of my children. Susan, my youngest daughter, started buying Dad's work on eBay in 2002—she has 172 pieces, some one-of-a kind. My son Bob has designed his home to showcase his grandfather's art and also has a huge personal collection. My daughter Sally has many antique pieces, but also collects the newer reproductions, as well. Her personal 'museum' contains a great many of my father's original drawings of production pieces. All five of my children are avid collectors of their grandfather's artwork and their homes attest to that. Everything is in the Till Goodan trust to be jointly managed by them and by their mutual agreement, so that the extensive body of work will not be broken up."

Wallace China Restored

True West Home 2000–Current

Texas manufacturer True West Home began in Dallas, Texas, in 2001, a business acquisition by noted interior design professional Mark Clay. Clay purchased the company from author and entrepreneur, Tyler Beard and his wife Teresa, who had actually revived the Wallace "Rodeo" pattern earlier in 1991 on his own. At that time, the collection was made by the H.F. Coors Company, a maker of vitreous restaurant-quality china, which was then located in Los Angeles. Beard had moved ahead with the idea and ran the business up until he decided to devote himself full time to his writing efforts and let it go.

New owner Clay hired Pat Turner, a long-time friend of Beard, to help run the company. Their first order of business was to contact Betty Goodan, who was glad to be involved with the new effort. She worked with them to reinstate a quality, licensed reproduction of her father's designs. They continued production with Coors, who was capable of manufacturing an almost perfect match to the 1940s original. The current H.F. Coors factory owner, Dirck Schou, believes they have come as close to the original product as manufacturing processes allow, continuing to serve a growing number of satisfied retailers.

True West Home "Christmas" pattern, based on original artwork by Till Goodan in the 1950s. The newest design, authorized by Betty Goodan, is one of the best sellers in True West's offerings today. (Courtesy True West Home)

Above: The effect of "Pioneer Trails" by Wallace China, circa 1950, in blue glaze on white is fresh and striking, a beautiful version of this exceptional set. Artist Till Goodan.
Right: Vintage Wallace China, "The 49ers," serving or steak platter. Shows twenty-hitch mule team in orange brown glaze on white, a rare image anywhere. Artist unknown.
Far right: By True West Home—"Westward Ho," Christmas Pattern—original Till Goodan art on a cup. Here, a cowboy dragging a tree back to the ranch is thrown from his horse. One can only imagine the rest.

Across the Decades with Wallace China

Wallace China dinnerware

"Over fifty years ago, my father, Till Goodan, designed four patterns in dinnerware named 'Rodeo,' 'Boots & Saddle,' 'Pioneer Trails,' and 'Longhorn,' all of which have become vintage dinnerware highly sought by collectors of western china.

Betty Goodan Andrews, an all-American daughter of the West: cowgirl, artist, mother, historian—keeper of the flame.

"In 1991, the 'Rodeo' pattern was reproduced by True West. It enjoyed great success, although no credit was given to my father's beautiful artwork. Now, Mark Clay, the new owner of True West Home, is honoring my father by reproducing a second design called 'Boots & Saddle.'

"Since I inherited the Till Goodan estate, I was able to provide all of the original artwork including Dad's distinctive signature. This quality china is being made, with careful attention to authenticity, right here in the United States. My father, being the consummate American cowboy, would be very pleased.

"I am also happy that, with my blessing, the Till Goodan name will appear in its rightful place on the 'Rodeo' china. I am looking forward to seeing my father's treasure trove of artwork appearing again as a tribute to his portrayal of the Old West that he so enjoyed."

Wild horse round-up cup from "Westward Ho—Rodeo" pattern, artist Till Goodan, originally by Wallace China, made by True West Home.

In 2003, the new True West Home headquarters moved to Royse City, where Turner runs the day-to-day operations. A year later, they added the "Westward Ho—Boots & Saddle," "Longhorn," and Christmas pattern, a new motif based on a Goodan Christmas card, to their production.

According to Turner, "True West Home is committed to maintaining the quality and copyrighted images of the original Wallace 'Westward Ho' patterns and all of Till Goodan's designs." They intend to guarantee that the new products will have the same kind of heirloom status for the future.

Both oven and dishwasher proof, these collections are delighting a new generation of customers. Western retailers, dude ranches, and consumers nationwide love its homespun warmth and charm. Till Goodan's legacy will have a long and enduring future.

Vernon Kilns
1939–1989

By the early 1950s, the West Coast had gained recognition for having some of the most successful ceramic production in the country. Ceramic tiles, restaurant and residential dinnerware, and numerous decorative objects owed their thanks to the rich clays found throughout the state. Vernon Kilns pottery of Vernon, California, was just one producer among them.

Established originally in 1912 as Paxon China, the company was renamed and taken under new leadership in 1939, and it succeeded in becoming one of the most prolific producers of dinnerware and giftware in the nation. Using adhesive type ball clay with glazes made of California-based silica, Vernon Kilns was well known for quality specialty ware, and especially as experts in the transfer print process.

A series of fires in the 1940s almost destroyed the pottery, but the factory was rebuilt and resumed its place

Incredibly realistic image with skilled painting under the glaze by artist Paul Davidson. Part of "Winchester '73" collection by Vernon Kilns, 1950s. Also known as "Frontier Days."

in the market. Demand for California pottery was high. But when the foreign imports hit America in the late '50s, Vernon Kilns sold out to a company called Metlox, who continued to market the product under the name Vernonware until 1989.

By 1940, the golden age of Western film and the celluloid cowboy had emerged full blown as Hollywood took on the role of preserving the myth of our favorite hero. Few Americans realize that the last cattle drive in the West took place in 1895, and the cowboy as a freewheeling nomad ended his free-range rambles before the turn of the century. But the film world and television serials would keep the myth alive, fueled with a wealth of screenwriters and actors who recreated the bigger than life cowboy.

Vernon Kilns would create one of the most remarkable ceramic collections ever during the 1940s and '50s, commemorating archetypal scenes out of the Frontier West. The design "Bits of the Old West" was created by a staff artist known simply as Cavett. These decals were then hand-colored under the glaze in brilliant shades of translucent blues, yellows, and reds.

"Bits of the Old West" collection by Vernon Kilns. Shown is "The Fleecing," one of eight different plates—we all recognize the scene of the dishonest card player.
Detail: Powerful facial expressions by master artist Cavett, hand-painted under the glaze.

We learn about Cavett from Maxine Feek Nelson in *Collectible Vernon Kilns*: "Early in the 1940s, a young Mr. Cavett (no one remembered his first name) had his art career cut short when he took a leave of absence from his job at Vernon Kilns to join the military. He was killed while training for the paratroopers. He is best known for the very popular 'Bit Plate' series, most of which carry his name in the lower right-hand corner of the picture. An exception is the 'Bits of the Old Northwest' series by E. Fortier."

The line debuted in the early 1940s and was produced until 1953. It became a popular collector's series, just one of seven by Vernon Kilns that divided the United States into regions. ("Bits of New England," "Bits of the Southwest," etc.). The highly detailed images of life in the Old West included "The Horse Thieves," "The Train Robbers," "The Stage Arrival," "The Stage Robbers," "The Bar Fly," "The Fleecing," "The Posse," and "Horse Taming."

In keeping with the technology of the day, the images were transferred via copper plates onto transfer paper and fired, then color was added before the final glaze. Based on the plates in the author's collection (seven out of eight in total), the colors have remained flawless and the top glaze crackle-free to this day. The detail and expression in the characters are remarkable, evoking a marvelous sense of nostalgia. This collection is Cavett's legacy.

Probably the best known Western-themed collection made by Vernon Kilns was the group created in the

Top: "Winchester '73," an astonishing feat of decoration, a bronco bucks around this small egg holder. (Courtesy Janet Hix)
Middle: "Winchester '73" butter dish and cover with stagecoach, another masterpiece by Vernon Kilns. (Janet Hix photo and collection)
Bottom: "Winchester '73" carafe with lid, a most prized piece shows steam engine locomotive. (Janet Hix photo and collection)

and round-ups—the West remembered and imagined, a marvelous gallery of images.

In June of 1950, Universal Pictures International released the film *Winchester '73*. It starred Jimmie Stewart and Shellie Winters, among others. The dinnerware was developed as part of the marketing, and theaters that showed the film promoted department stores that sold the dinnerware.

According to *The Best of Collectible Dinnerware* by Jo Cunningham, one print ad stated the following: "All the romance of the winning of the West in this attractive new palette, designed with a 1950s known as "Winchester '73," after the rifle of the same name and the ensuing Universal Pictures film.

Artist Paul Davison worked for Vernon Kilns most of his career and left a museum-worthy series of illustrations to tell our epic Western story. Background glazes of "Winchester '73" seem to vary, depending on the production, and pieces range from creamy white, gray, or even with an ecru or greenish cast. On the various plates, casseroles, chop platters, dinner and salad dishes, cups and saucers, mugs and more, the artist created transfers of firearms, cowboys, buffalo hunts, campfires, wild horses, Longhorns,

Top: Wyoming State plate. Orpha Klinker developed and illustrated this line from Vernon Kilns with a clear vision of each state's emblems. Her skill was remarkable.

Right: Washington State plate. Another good example of Orpha Klinker's ability to organize subject, shape and line.

particular appeal to the masculine taste for causal dining anytime, anywhere. Winchester '73 has a Western appeal with its bold scenes, cowboys and covered wagons."

According to Vernon Kilns' historian and author, Maxine Feek Nelson, trouble arose, however, in January of 1953, due to a conflict with the Winchester Arms Corporation over the unlicensed use of the name. The title of the collection was soon changed to "Frontier Days," and collectors have learned to look for it either way.

Among the many commemorative and assorted gift items in Vernon Kilns' catalogs were the many state plates, produced from 1950 to 1956, as gift or souvenir items, either in brown or blue on a white background. These spanned all existing fifty states. Vernon Kilns commissioned artist Orpha Klinker (1891–1964), who was best known for her historical subjects, and she made remarkable compositions of state historical data in her renderings.

Classically trained at the American International Academy in Washington, D.C., and widely collected, Klinker brought the best of each state's history to the series. Her ability to capture Western subjects is obvious in her highly detailed compositions shown on the Washington and Wyoming examples. She was skilled at depicting landscape, Native Americans, and above all, the bronco, a powerful icon that conveys a clear and romantic Western message.

Vernon Kilns pottery continues to circulate and accrue in value. The artists they chose made these products among the finest in the genre.

Frankoma Pottery

1927–Current

Unique among my entire collection is the handsome and colorful clay dinnerware by Frankoma of Oklahoma, one of the Midwest's most respected potteries. One of the patterns shown, the once popular "Wagon Wheel," remains as an example of remarkable handcrafting and mass production, since the strength of its design is made in the mold. Yet, each and every piece is unique because of the glazing technique. It's the kind of pottery that's hard to imagine wasn't actually made one individual piece at a time.

The beautiful prairie green glaze, as well as the desert gold color (not shown) both have exceptional depth, warmth, and variegation, putting them in a class all their own. The "Wagon Wheel" series is a rich collection, from vegetable bowls and covered casseroles, to a variety of mugs, plates, platters, and cups, as well as a salt and pepper set, teapot, creamer, sugar bowl, and water pitcher. Although the design is vintage, it feels contemporary, with shapes that speak to our modern way of living.

Together, the dinnerware is rich in presentation and full of character, a beautiful tableware to use and enjoy. Not specifically Western, "Wagon Wheel" nonetheless belongs

"Wagon Wheel" Ranch collection by Frankoma Pottery: Understated in form and finish, this hearty pottery is endearing and warm, beautiful to look at and use.

to the overland experience, to the many pioneers who preceded us. It's a perfect symbol of the American West.

"Ranch," a newer series that is still being manufactured, takes off on the enduring brand tradition, with glazes highlighting the brands in contrasting colors around the rim. The raised brands and Longhorns give a terrific three-dimensional effect, and the beauty of the intense opaque glazes in bone, navy, forest green, and red are spectacular.

John Frank, the founder of Frankoma, came to Norman, Oklahoma, in 1927 and took a faculty post at the University of Oklahoma. In addition, he opened his own studio to make his own creations. As an artist, he was inspired by the world around him, and his vessels and functional shapes are organic and natural in feeling. His glazes were based on the colors of the earth—its minerals and its ores.

Within a short time, Frank realized his future was in making clay objects, and the company was started in earnest, dedicated to making "beautiful pottery for everyday living." In Frank's own words, "the clay carries a piece of each person who touches it. There is something about the clay which holds on to the spirit of the eight to ten artisans who handle each piece." He refused to hire anyone who didn't love their job. The staff at Frankoma today still feels the same way.

Kandy Steeples, an employee at Frankoma for over thirty years, says most customers are stunned when they go through the factory.

"They just can't believe what they're seeing. Everything here is done just the way it was back in the 1930s. Our product is hand poured, hand trimmed, and hand glazed. There's no automated machinery to stamp things out. Everything is hand crafted. Once you're involved, and see a product transformed, you actually feel like you're a part of it."

Master mold maker Lacy Green turning a mountain air canister on the potter's wheel. Every Frankoma piece is worked on by human hands.

The original business remained in the family for some years following Frank's death, and has had various owners until recently. Joe Ragosta, who wanted to preserve a local tradition, took over in 2008.

From the time Frank started creating dinnerware in Norman, to the factory in Sapulpa, Oklahoma, local clays were utilized. By 1954, when the clay they had started with was depleted, they switched to clays found just a few miles from the factory. According to the company's website, "raw clay is cleaned and processed to form a rich, dark gray clay that is formed by individual craftsmen into the finished shapes. Each piece is individually hand-trimmed to remove rough edges and ensure that the detail shows properly. After the first trip through the kiln, the clay develops its signature terra cotta color. Each piece is then glazed individually in one of our Frankoma colors. Most pieces are then brushed to remove glaze from some areas so that the beautiful terra cotta color will show through. The pieces are then fired a second time to create a permanent piece of artwork. It's microwaveable, dishwasher safe, and oven proof."

Fortunately for the collector and a new generation of users, the current operation is one of the last remaining potteries in the United States to offer a truly American handcrafted product. Although "Wagon Wheel" isn't currently in production, new designs that are both functional and decorative beckon the consumer, and an onsite museum, as well as the factory, are open for tours.

"Ranch" collection: A much later addition, simple and attractive in its saturated colors and bold finish. (Courtesy Frankoma Pottery)

The 1950s

Possibly the most satirized decade of the twentieth-century, the 1950s saw shifts in mainstream American values and habits. Post-war babies grew up in a prospering America, the sons and daughters of parents who had suffered the Great Depression and never wanted their children to know hunger or deprivation. The American home became a showcase for new technology and appliances, and the American mother its queen.

Teens had a rebel without a cause in anti-hero Marlon Brando (*The Wild One*), who encouraged a new kind of independence. Smoking, drinking, and sex were part

Left: Themed lunch boxes made of tin or aluminum were all the rage from the 1940s through the '60s featuring Disney or television characters, Westerns especially. They're all vintage collectibles today.
Above: Horse clock—cast lead with golden finish (or bronze patina) by United Products, circa 1950s.
Bottom left: Covered wagon ceramic liqueur decanter by Paul Lux Creations, circa 1960s.

Right: Steve Weil, President of Rockmount Ranch Wear, in his Denver retail store. Below: Rockmount Ranch Wear vintage Western shirt No. 6755, 1940s era.

of the newly born rock'n'roll generation. Against the atmosphere of cold war paranoia, science fiction was a big draw in literature and film, and Alfred Hitchcock created the first psycho thriller.

Fashion took its inspiration from rock'n'roll, Elvis Presley, and Brando. Men wore white T-shirts, black leather jackets, white socks, and ducktail haircuts. Girls wore full skirts, cuffed jeans, and tight sweaters. An overt oppressed sexuality pervaded the '50s, along with an urban bohemianism as suburban cocktail parties, Freud, and the automobile culture changed the way people dated, behaved, and even ate their food.

At home in the suburbs, the new electronic god, television, reigned over all other entertainment activities, with variety programming, comedy, and serials. The Swanson Company invented the TV dinner, pre-frozen and ready to eat in twenty-five minutes, and TV trays were invented so you could eat in the living room.

Not only does this image show a chuck wagon but also the camp cook ringing the triangle to call the cowboys in. On the far right, a cowboy on horseback waves in the background. On the inside of the rim is a cluster of cooking utensils and an ax embedded in a log. Back stamp reads "Syracuse C, Econo-Rim 2-Y (1944)."

This charming tin tray portrays a bucking bronco—a perfect TV or snack tray. Circa 1950. (Courtesy Pat Turner, True West Home)

Would Western china be threatened by these aluminum tray dinner replacements? Not on your life. Roy Rogers launched his television serial in 1951, and Gene Autry shortly thereafter. Next, Westerns created for adults, like *Maverick,* filled the nightly programming. Soon, some of the most famous, longest running shows in history, like *Gunsmoke,* took hold. The china industry experienced its golden years in terms of the Western genre. Most vintage Western collectibles date from this decade.

Tepco China Company

1918–1968

Tepco is considered by many to be second in popularity as a Western china collectible after Wallace China. An acronym for the Technical Porcelain and Chinaware Company, the Tepco company produced five memorable Western patterns that can mix-and-match well with each other or stand alone. The dinnerware in all its variety was vitrified china destined for hotel and restaurant use, as well as for the U.S. Marines—widely stocked on ship's galleys during World War II.

The most widely used of Tepco's Western-themed dinnerware was "Branding Irons," easily recognizable by its tan body and center motif consisting of a saddle, roping cowboys, broncos, brands, or hats, with an unusual oxen-yoke around the rim. It's interesting to note that true Tepco Ware, often imitated, has a curious detail—the brands have letters on their ends and, when read from left to right, spell the word "Tepco."

The second pattern celebrating the Old West was called "Western Traveler" and was based on the legendary Pony Express. The Pony Express riders carried mail across the West for eighteen months during

"Branding Irons" dinner plate with saddle, circa 1940s–'50s. The brands spell the word Tepco.

A sample of the "Branding Irons" vitreous china by one of America's most prolific producers, Tepco, circa 1950s. This place setting would have turned any common diner into a 5-star restaurant for me. (Photo by Lindsay Allen)

the Civil War. The service was disbanded in 1861, when the nationwide telegraph system was completed. Soon after, the completion of the transcontinental railroad in 1869 assured that mail would be delivered safely to points West. But the Pony Express riders were a daring bunch that left an indelible imprint.

The center motif of the plate shows the changing of horses—that moment where the relay of riders meets up to take a fresh mount. The border design shows stagecoaches before a panorama of mountains. All the patterns were affixed via the transfer decal method, where the backing is burned away during firing and the image is fused into the china. Nothing is known about the artist who designed them.

Three other Western patterns, "Wagon Wheel," "Ox Head," and an "Early California" series, can be found in circulation as well.

According to careful research by Janet Hix, the artist for this line was Californian Ken Bemis, circa 1950s. This series is a rare and hard to find remnant of the era.

All Tepco china surfaces were fired under the glaze with a two-fire process, making them durable and hard (vitreous china). With the exception of a few scratches or knife marks, the vintage pieces in my collection appear to have survived in remarkable condition.

A catalog page from the 1950s, courtesy of *The Best of Collectible Dinnerware* by Jo Cunningham, lists the following items in the Tepco "Branding Irons" collection: Baking dishes, bouillon bowls, butter dishes, coffee cups with handles, egg cups, saucers, compotes, fruit bowls, grapefruit dishes, mugs, mustard dishes, plates in eight sizes, soup bowls, grill plates, chop plates, platters in ten sizes, pitchers, tea pots, sugar bowls, sauce boats, salad plates in seven sizes, salt and pepper shakers, *bain marie* jars, ash trays, and ice tubs!

Tepco was located in El Cerrito, California, and was established in 1918 by John Pagliero and his wife Dolores. It reached its heyday in the 1940s and '50s, and was capable of turning out some 30,000 dishes per day. The factory closed its doors in 1968, a family business that lasted through two world wars and two generations. Its distribution reached across California and beyond, making them one of the largest manufacturers in the U.S. in the early part of the twentieth century. They eventually had branch offices in Houston, Seattle, and Los Angeles.

According to an article on Tepco Ware in *American Craft* by Joseph Heaven, dated 1982, family diners, cafes, and restaurants were still serving off this ware in California up until the 1980s.

Left: "Western Traveler" by Tepco. Pony Express riders exchanging horses on the run. Above: Note the different color clay bodies on these five pieces, obviously made at different times during the 1940s and '50s. The Pony Express was a wonderful subject to be used as decoration. Artist unknown.

Syracuse China

1871–2009

Although the tableware made by Syracuse China bearing Western motifs is estimated to have been produced from the 1940s to the '60s, this venerable china manufacturer had a long and rich history that followed America through the war years, the technological innovations of mass production in the china manufacturing industry, and the shift from rail travel to air. According to *Restaurant China* by Barbara Conroy, one out of every five to ten pieces of commercial china found in the U.S. secondary market has a Syracuse back stamp.

Syracuse began as the Onondaga Pottery Company in 1871 in Syracuse, New York, a consortium of sixteen potteries. According to author Cleota Reed in her book *Syracuse China,* Onondaga was the name of the county in which Syracuse was located, named after the Native American Iroquois tribe of the area. The group's intent was to create tableware for restaurants, hotels, clubs, hospitals, and railway and ship lines.

Onondaga first used the Syracuse China mark in 1895 to mark the pure white vitreous china for which

Syracuse China: Beautiful enough to be a collector plate but more likely restaurant or possibly railroad china—numerous knife marks on plate. Decal shows pioneers fording a river. Back stamp indicates production date 1964.

Syracuse China: Scalloped edges and airbrushed stencil—a distinguished image, 1967.

Quality vintage restaurant ware, rust glaze on tan body. A small bread and butter plate with airbrushed ten-gallon hat and fluted rim. Made by Syracuse China, 1951.

they were one of the first and foremost American manufacturers. More than half a century later, in 1966, it reincorporated as the Syracuse China Corporation. Soon after, the company purchased the Mayer China Company of Beaver Falls, Pennsylvania, and in 1987, it took over the legendary Shenango China in New Castle. Finally, Syracuse China became a subsidiary of Pfaltzgraff until 1995, when they in turn sold the company to Libby of Toledo, Ohio. It was with a certain amount of wistfulness that after 138 years of production Syracuse China closed its doors in April of 2009, ending its run as an American original.

During its long history, various trade names were found on the tableware, such as Adobe Ware (tan body), Airlite, Castleton, Econo Rim, Old Ivory, Shell Edge, Silhouette, Syralite, and Trend, with a modern rounded square shape. Over the years, Syracuse managed to guide the vitrified china business in special ways. All the way back in 1885, they perfected what Americans had long been striving for—a semi-porcelain china that would withstand abuse and look beautiful, something even better than ironstone.

By 1890, they had perfected a fully vitrified china capable of being made in a two-step firing process. In 1896, they introduced a new type of hotel ware with an innovative and highly practical rolled edge, adding to the durability and usefulness of every plate, a feature that practically became the standard.

Among its many artists and artisans, no decorating method was left untried—from hand painting to transfer prints and decals, the use of platinum and gold burnishing, stripes and bands, and a myriad of other

On April 9, 2009, after 138 years of production, Libby Inc. decided to shut down the Syracuse China factory production of Syracuse China and move it from North America. At that time, the plant had 275 employees.

On the last day of production, each employee was given a commemorative plate with a montage of images from throughout the company's history including eight historic company logos. The face of the plate states, "Though the world may change around us, our history remains the same."

The back of each plate was stamped "38-A," the last date stamp to appear on a Syracuse China product made in Syracuse. The "38" is code for the year it was made—1971, the company's centennial year, plus 38 years. The "A" stands for the first quarter of the year. The back of each plate also has text indicating it was one of the last "pieces to be made in Syracuse, N.Y."

The archives and china collections were donated to the Onondaga Historical Association.

—www.SyracuseChina.com

"Sundown," a very popular and highly collectible restaurant china by Syracuse, circa 1960s, with cowboys singing around the fire. (Photo of Roy Rogers courtesy Fred Goodwin, Concept Productions)

decorative applications. Even stencil and airbrush were applied from the 1930s on.

As trends changed and the growing workforce took women out of the home and into the workplace, more eateries serving that workforce were needed. Syracuse was there as a multi-billion dollar industry ready to serve the new commercial and institutional foodservice operations that had a high demand for dinnerware. Although once makers of fine residential china, by 1970 the company manufactured for restaurant use only.

Numerous innovations can be credited to Syracuse, and in particular a streamlined shape known as Econo Rim, introduced in the late '30s to conserve space on railway car dining tables, and a clay body known as Syralite, a strong and durable medium-gauge ware introduced in 1964.

Collectors tend to focus on the early years of production, especially hotel and restaurant ware.

Above: Syracuse China, "Emigration to the Western Country," also made in the 1960s. Plate measures only 4.75 x 4.75 inches. Right: Airbrushed decorative work was a specialty. Warm caramel glaze and rust colored rim are very appealing. All plate edges have some kind of decorative lip or surface treatment. Dates range from 1951 to1953 (brand saucer by Jackson China).

Shenango China
1901–1992

Lavish detail and highly illustrative scenes of the Old West adorn the samples from Shenango, which made its bid at the Western craze in the 1950s through the early '60s. The collection of restaurant ware shown here, dated from that period, is in pristine condition. The campfire scene on the steak platter is extremely well done, with every detail of clothing and gear picked out (artist unknown).

The clay bodies of these samples are either tan or off-white, and all have the rim roll, or double roll, on the back that added strength to the plate and allowed for stacking without scratching.

Above: Shenango China's "Western Round-Up" Ranch Ware steak platter, a fully detailed rendering.
Right: Back stamp of another Shenango China division, Inca Ware—a beautiful image.

Shenango started back in 1901, and by 1912 it had acquired the old New Carlisle Pottery plant in New Castle, Pennsylvania, and moved there. A subsidiary called Castleton China was formed in 1941 specifically to manufacture china for Rosenthal of Germany. That subsidiary was sold in 1951.

Three pieces showing cowboys at work. Back stamp says "Rim Rol." Good example of white vitreous heavy duty restaurant ware.

Wallace China of California actually became a subsidiary of Shenango in 1951 and produced some of its commercial ware in Los Angeles before it was closed down. Shenango and all of its subsidiaries, including Mayer China, were purchased in 1968 by the Interpace Corporation. Syracuse China then took over with a buyout in 1987, and it ended production entirely by 1992. Shenango is currently considered a Syracuse China company brand name.

According to Conroy's *Restaurant China,* "Shenango was America's largest manufacturer of food service china until the 1980s. They were known for medium- to heavy-gauge vitrified ware. The company used transfer prints, stencil airbrush, lines and bands, hand-painted decorations, solid underglaze color, colored glaze, and decals. Trade names included Carlton, Citation, Gala, and Inca Ware, among others."

They also patented Wel Roc, a type of construction with a raised area under the well of the plate to reduce the chance of cracking.

Mayer China

1888–1990

With roots as far back as the late 1800s, Mayer China is yet another of the collectible restaurant china manufacturers that survived over a century of production. It was founded as Mayer Pottery in 1888, later to become Mayer China in 1923. The company became a subsidiary of Shenango China in 1964, and both were taken over by Interpace Corporation in 1968. Yet another takeover put Mayer China into private hands until 1984, when Syracuse took over the operation. In 1990,

Mayer China restaurant ware featuring Longhorns and brands on white heavy-duty service. Sophisticated and simple. Circa 1960s.

X-L relish dish. The commission is unknown, but it's an effective and simple design. Back stamp reads "Inca Ware, New Castle Pennsylvania." Also "Rim-rol."

Mayer China, circa 1940–1950, airbrushed round-up scene. Backstamp reads "Mayer China, Beaver Falls, Ivory 354."

Mayer as a separate entity ceased to exist. In part, production continued under the name Beaver Falls and later on as Royal Monarch.

Dinnerware by Mayer was typically off-white in color, with ivory and tan bodies by the 1930s. Clientele included a wide range of transportation companies, and U.S. military operations. One of its nicest patterns shows a Longhorn with brands.

The unusual airbrushed design of a cattle round up shown here dates from around the 1940s.

Jackson China

1917–1987

Jackson China was yet another of the major potteries to supply the military, railroad, and air and ship lines of the twentieth century. With a long history that began in 1917 in Falls Creek, Pennsylvania, the company was founded by Harry Jackson in the heart of the pottery manufacturing area of America. It was later sold to an English manufacturer, and finally purchased by Delco Tableware International before its demise. The dinnerware can be identified by the names of Jackson Vitrified China Company, Jackson China, or finally Jackson China Marketing, an entity that lasted from 1981 to 1987.

According to Conroy's *Restaurant China,* "Jackson produced medium- to heavy-gauge vitrified china for hotels, restaurants, clubs, schools, and transportation industries. Ware was produced in blue from the 1930s to the '40s; pink, tan (called Jac Tan) from the 1930s through the 60s, and later with ivory and white bodies. In the later years, 1960 through 1985, the company specialized in custom commercial china, a focus which was reflected on their back stamp from 1973."

In the late 1980s, their upscale "Maitré d Collection" was manufactured in England and their best upscale line, "Royal Jackson," a fine-gauge bone china commercial ware, was produced at the Elizabethan Fine Bone China plant, also in England. Surface decoration included single, multicolor, or metallic lines and bands, and stencil airbrushed designs in one or more colors, solid color glaze, custom transfer prints and decals, and, of course, some hand painting.

Whoever designed their Western collection had a grand sense of style. The pieces date from the late 1950s and early '60s. The hats and broncos and various designs are bold and simple and fitting for Western tables. The plates, cups, and bowls were suitable for the kind of commercial abuse that restaurants or dude ranches surely would have inflicted.

Left: Jackson China, circa 1950s. The grill plate is especially nice. A hat, pistol, and saddle make this a Western treasure.

Above: Cowboy on bronco based on an etching made for Jackson China circa 1950 by Henry Zeigler (1889–1968), famed New York artist, reportedly raised in Texas. Partially glazed rim is an artistic touch.

Buffalo China (Oneida)

1901–1983

Founded in 1901, Buffalo Pottery, as it was first called, was established to create premiums to be given away with laundry soap. The founder, John D. Larkin, probably never dreamed his company would become one of the three largest commercial producers of custom hotel ware in America.

Automated and renovated throughout the decades, Buffalo Pottery became Buffalo China by 1956, and began to expand by adding a subsidiary, Allegheny China of Pennsylvania. A supplier to the U.S. military during the war years, it also had numerous railroads and various restaurants as its customers.

Throughout the 1960s and '70s, the firm continued to grow under the leadership of the founder's grandson, Harold Esty, Jr. Methods applied to vitreous china included the full range of screening, printing, and glaze applications. As many as fourteen different trade names identify the various colored china bodies. Buffalo invented the technique of two body colors, with one color laminated over the other. The end product was marketed under the trade name "Lamelle."

In 1983, Buffalo China became a subsidiary of Oneida Ltd. of Oneida, New York.

Top: Restaurant ware with bronco, possibly for Silver Saddle Restaurants, which are located in Idaho, California, and Arizona. There are dozens of establishments today with this name but getting to the root of this vintage piece proved difficult.

Left: This item of table service is rarely seen anymore. How many restaurants do you know that use a relish dish today?

Homer Laughlin China Company

1871–Current

If any single manufacturer belongs to every decade of Western china production, it would be the Homer Laughlin China Company. They have persisted in the face of tough times and tougher competition, and creatively evolved to serve the consumer's needs and wants in both the commercial and residential market.

Restaurant ware dated from 1969. Homer Laughlin pattern #1837 simply called "Cowboys." The pattern was in the company's general line and commonly sold to steak houses and other Western-themed restaurants.

"Rhythm" by Homer Laughlin. All pieces were designed in 1954 for F.W. Woolworth Company depicting cowboy life—a homestead, a roping cowboy, and a campfire cook-out on one of their most popular and contemporary shapes. Salt and pepper shakers, courtesy Julie Rose & Company, manufactured in 2009. (Photo by Lindsay Allen)

According to company resources, their long history began in Liverpool, Ohio, in 1871, with the Laughlin brothers, Homer and Shakespeare, who sold dinnerware purchased from other manufacturers. In 1873, they built a plant and began production of white ware, a growing demand. By 1880, under the leadership (by that time) solely of Homer, the company had become firmly established as a respected maker of ceramic dinnerware.

The company expanded, went through successive ownerships, and moved across the river to Newell, West Virginia, where by 1912 the four plants could produce a staggering 300,000 pieces of ware per day. By 1914, five separate plants had been built, giving the company a total of 78 ware kilns and 60 decorating kilns. With the advent of a significant invention in the pottery industry, the continuously firing kiln, the Homer Laughlin China Company was among the first to revolutionize the manufacture of their entire product line.

In 1923, they built yet another new plant with this modern innovation and gradually upgraded several of the other plants to make them more efficient. The 1930s and '40s saw new leadership and energy under the design direction of Frederick Rhead, who remained with the company until 1942. These were pivotal years for the company that were enriched by new methods of application, new shapes and patterns, and especially the creation of "Fiesta Ware," the colorful dinnerware that has been adored by America since its inception. After World War II, production reached a peak in 1948, when some three thousand workers produced over 120 million pieces of ware annually!

The 1950s through the '90s were marked by the increase in dinnerware made offshore at little cost. Many potteries didn't survive, but the Homer Laughlin company shifted its market to cater to the hotel and restaurant trade and in 1959 introduced their "best china"—band vitrified hotel china. The shift proved to be a wise move and sustained them through the tough market years of the '60s and '70s.

In the late 1980s, production turned to lead-free china, a big priority for the environmentally aware. "Fiesta" was reintroduced in updated colors and attracted a new generation. As "Fiesta" flourished in the retail sector and the company

"Home on the Range" produced sometime in the 1990s, restaurant china by Homer Laughlin that echoes the past.

According to Jo Cunningham in her book *Homer Laughlin China, 1940s and 50s,* the "Rhythm" shape was designed by Don Schreckengost in 1950 at the request of Henry Lindquist, a buyer for the Woolworth Company who was looking for an entirely new shape. The new coupe shape was called "Rhythm" and its styling and techniques of production were different than any previously used methods.

"Rhythm" was the first shape designed for and made entirely on the automatic jigger. It can be found in ivory, decorated and undecorated, as well as in solid colors like yellow, gray, chartreuse, dark green, and burgundy. It was sold to many distributors and used in "Dura Print" combinations.

soared ahead in the food service china industry, the plants themselves underwent massive upgrades and improvement. Leadership meanwhile was being passed down through the second, third, and fourth generations of management, and in June of 2002, Joe Wells III was elected president and CEO.

Said Wells, "The mission of the Homer Laughlin China Company remains the same as it always has been. We will continue to focus on our core products—domestically produced and decorated quality and lead-free china for the retail and commercial markets."

Detail of pasta bowl made by Homer Laughlin, "Rhythm" series (see page 160). Classic scene of cowboys around the campfire.

The charming Western ware shown here was made on the very popular, and at that time contemporary, "Rhythm" style clay body, made in the 1950s for the F.W. Woolworth Company, one of the company's biggest customers. The various decals depict a roping cowboy, a homestead, and a campfire scene.

The group "Home on the Range," produced between 1990 and 2000, is a callback to the earlier ware of the '50s that was once so popular.

It's remarkable to think that since its founding, the company has proudly produced over 35,000 china patterns.

Japan and Western Dinnerware

Late 1950s

It's impossible to write any history of American pottery without mentioning the Japanese, a culture and source of ceramic ware that flooded America's shores and reshaped an entire industry.

The art of ceramic making has been a huge part of Japanese handcraft for centuries. During the nineteenth and early twentieth centuries, exports to America were primarily the same products used by the Japanese—decorative items and tea pots, cups and dishes that looked typically Japanese.

According to *China and Glass in America, 1880–1980*, by the 1940s, Japan had become America's foremost foreign supplier of porcelain and earthenware dishes. In a count made in 1928, over seven thousand small and large potteries were sustaining employment in greater Japan. Imports to America reached such a point by 1930 that in 1933 President Roosevelt was asked by an association of American potteries to protect American producers of tableware from Japanese competition.

The attack on Pearl Harbor in 1941 put an end to Japanese exporting of china and glass during the war years. After the war ended, however, the production of pottery goods slowly shifted even more to the Pacific Rim. The Japanese were skilled at ceramic ware and mass production, and could make cheaper products in

Top: Milk cup—possibly one of the more endearing pottery items in this genre. (Cup courtesy Pat Turner, True West Home)
Above: A simple child's cup with a cowboy on a bucking horse, hand painted and air brushed on white clay. Other side shows Saguaro cactus.

large quantities. It took almost a full twenty years for the industry to regain its export production volume to the U.S. after the war, but as it did it brought American production to its knees.

By 1950, factories in the city of Nagoya, a pottery center focused on goods for the West, were reengineering their thinking to modify designs and shapes to please the tastes of Americans. By 1960, some 64 percent of imports of dinnerware were of Japanese origin.

Within another ten years, department store shelves were full of Japanese tableware, and popular women's magazines ran full-page ads for dishware by manufacturers like Noritake, Fitz and Floyd, Otagiri, and Mikasa, firms that were becoming well known and respected.

The many California potteries and those in the Ohio area were the hardest hit, and they slowly succumbed to the influx of imports. They began to close as the competition stole the market. In San Francisco, an enterprising marketing/distribution company contracted products in Japan under the name of Fred Roberts. They made decorative and utilitarian items in fanciful shapes. These were sold at quality department stores like Gump's in San Francisco, and are circulating widely on the collectors market today. The Western design work was apparently also done overseas, as the highly subjective and unusual designs seem to suggest.

Three patterns in particular made by Fred Roberts are included here. The actual date of production is uncertain. They may have been initiated in the late 1940s or early '50s. My favorite pattern has a Longhorn on a

Above: Utterly delightful, this Longhorn depiction had to have been made by a Japanese artist—the cow has very Asian eyes.
Left: Cup part of Fred Roberts set, plate shown on page 43.

divided grill plate surrounded by a border of brands. The Longhorn decal was obviously designed by someone who had never seen the animal in the flesh. The one on the plate has distinctly Asian features. But the stencils are highlighted by hand-applied brushwork and are quite charming and detailed.

Another producer was Nasco, or more fully, Nasco del Coronado. Little is available about this company, but it's another wonderful example of post-war Japanese Western. The interesting part of the Nasco ware is that every piece is hand painted over a stencil, be it a bronco, coffee pot, or covered wagon. Several different versions of the stencils appear to be used. Each item varies slightly and makes the collection an animated and wonderful group.

The market today imports products made in China, an aggressive competitor. Earlier in the twentieth century,

This strange plate came from a set of four with three other designs. I like it because it's so odd. The rider's costume evokes the Colonial period. It appears to have been drawn by someone who has never ridden a horse or seen a cowboy. Nasco Ware, made in Japan.

Nasco del Coronado covered wagon, bronco, and cookout scenes—every single plate is slightly different, all hand-painted with great freedom over the decals, circa 1950s. One of my very favorites and still in circulation—often found in full sets if you're lucky.

the blanks made for Japanese artisans were often made in China, to be decorated by the Japanese in a European, Asian, or American style, depending upon the customer. Other countries involved in china manufacture are Indonesia and Korea. You can never be too sure where your Western-themed tableware comes from. But if you want "Made in America," it's still here.

Above: Poor Japanese copy of Wallace originals, circa 1950s.
Right: Platter "Westward Ho" (Till Goodan), True West Home.

The 1960s

The 1960s were like a troubled adolescence, full of opposing forces and emotional turmoil. It was a time of change, when the establishment was being undermined by a visible revolution, a counterculture seeking new perspective in values and self-expression. The cultural revolution reacted to the excess of the 1950s, to its indulgence and flamboyance, to its corporate growth and conformity.

Third longest running Western after *Gunsmoke*, the TV series *Bonanza* ran 14 seasons, or 430 episodes. It began in September of 1959 and ran until 1973. It starred Lorne Greene as Ben; Pernell Roberts as Adam; Dan Blocker as Hoss (or Eric); Michael Landon as Little Joe; and David Canary as Candy, ranch foreman. The brothers were from different wives from the thrice widowed Ben. The story line focused on family relations, neighbors, and the land. (Courtesy Bob Anderson, *Trail Dust* magazine)
Leather panel by Silver King Silversmiths

Instead of conforming, a new youth movement tuned in and dropped out. It was the beginning of the drug culture, the hallucinogenic world of Timothy Leary and LSD. It was Haight-Ashbury and the growth of communes. The '60s saw Woodstock and the Beatles, the birth of Motown, the rise of folk music, and the import of British rock'n'roll.

A youthful John F. Kennedy followed on the heels of Dwight D. Eisenhower and brought a new Camelot to Washington with an emphasis on patriotism and an expanding space program. Hope reigned with the peaceful vision of Martin Luther King; madness intruded with the insane cult of Charles Manson.

In the cities, a new Left was growing with an angry awareness on the part of minorities who saw that America wasn't the same for people of color. Many turned militant.

In the world of entertainment and popular culture, Elvis continued to wow audiences while sounds of the Beach Boys, the Bee Gees, and Jim Morrison's Doors rocked a new generation of listeners. Film brought us some of the all-time greats like *Lawrence of Arabia* and *The Graduate.* Producers of the Western searched for new ways to explore the West and delivered unforgettable characters seen in classics like *Midnight Cowboy, The Wild Bunch,* and *Butch Cassidy and the Sundance Kid.*

It was a weakened market for Westerns overall, however, and the film genre moved to Italy, where Sergio Leone made Clint Eastwood into an idol in *Fistful of Dollars, Last Man Standing,* and *The Good, the Bad, and the Ugly*. Alternative Westerns like *The Magnificent Seven* made the Western into an art film.

On the home front, the West barely surfaced in fashion or home décor. But a few dinnerware producers persisted in giving the marketplace what they thought it wanted or needed. Lucky for us.

Red Wing Art Pottery

1868–current

Of all the patterns in my collection, few are as fanciful as Red Wing's "Round-Up," introduced in 1955 and credited to designer Charles Murphy. The tab fleck glaze provides visual texture for the hand-painted designs, making each plate an original. The modern shapes are reminiscent of the work of noted ceramic designer Eva Zeisel, who helped create Red Wing's "Town and Country" line in 1946.

"Round-Up": This Red Wing setting feels like a day in the country. (Photo by Lindsay Allen)

Red Wing pottery is delightful piece by piece, and remarkable when seen as a whole collection. So colorful and festive. (Courtesy Sandy Couch)

Scenes on the various pieces of "Round-Up" are of cowboys branding, lassoing, or sitting on fences; the camp cook presiding next to the chuck wagon. The shapes of the clay body are called the "Casual" line and although a total of five different patterns use the "Round-up" shapes, none seem as distinctive as this. (The pattern is also sometimes called "Cowboy," as well as "Chuck Wagon.")

One of the collectors that I interviewed, Sandy Couch, adds this interesting provenance: "I found all of my pieces, about 120, in Arizona and Virginia, and have been collecting for fifteen to twenty years. I have tucked enough away to give to my grandsons someday, as they have great memories of eating on them! The long skinny bread tray became our hotdog or taco tray. Most prices have doubled during this time, but some have quadrupled. The only piece I have never found is the cruet set."

According to Sandy, each color was painted separately by a factory worker who had the glaze brush for just that one color. They stood in a line and individually applied the red, blue, tan, or yellow. It really makes sense when you look at each piece, as you can actually see the difference in style between colors.

As described in the book *Red Wing Art Pottery,* the company has a 142-year history that began in 1868, when a Mr. David Hallem began a stoneware factory in Red Wing, Minnesota, a clay rich area. The business was purchased locally and a corporation was formed called the Red Wing Stoneware Company, which grew to become a highly successful manufacturer.

Art pottery was introduced in the 1920s with a brushed ware line, and in the 1930s glazed ware, including dinnerware, was added with many new shapes and colors. The product focus shifted from an agrarian customer and functional items for farm use like crocks, jugs and storage vessels to a line for the homeowner including dinnerware, vases, ashtrays, and lamp bases.

The stoneware production ended in 1947, but art pottery continued until 1967 when market conditions made business impossible. The Gillmer family kept the business going as a sales company until they began manufacturing again in 1996. Scott Gillmer is the third generation of his family to run Red Wing Pottery. His grandfather started working there in the 1940s and became president in the 1950s.

Returning today to their craftsman roots, they now produce functional salt glaze pottery decorated with blue birds or flowers.

Nelson McCoy Pottery Company

1910–1990

The mid-1950s to mid-'60s brought us the remarkable Nelson McCoy collection known as "BarbeQue," or "El Rancho." It was solid, serviceable, and sculptural, covered with relief figures of cowboys, cattle skulls, and cacti, all created in the mold but highlighted with a wiped-off dark glaze. I consider it one of their greatest designs.

McCoy cookie jar, circa 1960. Opposite side shows covered wagon scene, both a powerful reminder of pioneer life.

The Nelson McCoy Pottery Company opened in 1910 in Roseville, Ohio, the beginning of a long and illustrious history. They were originally manufacturers of functional stoneware, especially jugs, jars, and crocks. But by the 1930s, the emphasis had changed to art pottery and other types of functional housewares like pedestals and umbrella stands. By then the name had changed to McCoy Sanitary Stoneware.

They survived the depression era by consolidating with a number of other potteries and forming American Clay Products. Later they changed their name back to Nelson McCoy Pottery. By the 1940s, thanks to a new designer, they were well known for their art pottery, especially planters. They survived World War II by doing contract work for the government and branching out into dinnerware and cookie jars, a category that has become highly collectible in recent years. In the end, competition from offshore manufacturing forced the company to cease production in 1990.

In its heyday in the 1940s through the '60s, all McCoy designs were conceived in-house, and the primary models were created in plaster. Then the molded objects would be shown to customers for feedback, an important part of deciding what would be produced. McCoy's true hallmark was the ability create functional items infused with creative design. By 1950, they had five hundred employees whose combined efforts produced 50,000 pieces of art ware, cookie jars, dinnerware, and florist ware every day, with at least fifty new designs annually.

The remarkable "El Rancho," or "BarbeQue" group, circa 1950s–1960, is a collection consisting of a coffee pot with a warming stand, mugs, a covered wagon serving dish with warming stand, a large bowl with a cowboy hat lid, which also served as a separate serving platter, and a beverage or ice tea jug (not shown). An added feature is the cookie jar. All are covered in the same off-white glaze with brown accents, finished with hand glazing and over-firing.

These contributions to the Western genre are exceptional, adding substance and style to what was truly an unmatchable example of workmanship at the mass-produced level.

McCoy ware. Seen as an ensemble, this is a museum-worthy collection, sculptural and rich in surface design. Large in scale, nice to hold, beautifully crafted.

Wellsville China
1933–1969

Ohio was home to a number of pottery works from the late nineteenth though the mid-twentieth century. Wellsville China operated from 1933 until 1969. In 1959, the nearby Sterling China Company took it over and continued manufacturing a variety of ware for restaurants and hotels. Shipping lines and various agencies of the U.S. government were their customers, as well.

The unusual plate with the fully drawn Western town on a tan stoneware body is an exceptional contribution to the Western genre. The scene depicts both a covered wagon and a stagecoach entering the main street, while cowboys are approaching from the opposite direction. A water trough in the middle of the street is in use by pack animals and mounted horses. A Wells Fargo Express and the Star Hotel flank the street, as well as a saloon. Various Indians and cowboys lounge on the boardwalk. The unique bird's eye view allows us to enter into this frontier town almost like an overhead movie camera.

The pieces shown are from a complete set, which includes cups and saucers, gravy boats, and platters. A partial scene on the salad plate is a detail from the dinner plate. Nothing is known about the artist who drew the original artwork, however, or why the series was made. Perhaps it had something to do with Wells Fargo. The stamp on the back indicates that the group was made during the early 1950s.

"Swingware" salad and dinner plates. From a full collection depicting a Western town.

Sterling China

1917–Current

Yet another china manufacturer in the Ohio area was Sterling China. Established in 1917 and still going strong, it's a successful family-owned business led by the third generation. By the mid-twentieth century, the company was touted as the third largest china manufacturer in America. Many customers were transportation systems—railroads in particular. In addition, they produced some of the highly distinctive and collectible ware designed by American home accessory designer Russel Wright throughout 1960.

In 1959, Sterling China purchased Wellsville China and continued operations there until 1969. As the company grew, it took over Crane China, a company in Puerto Rico, and changed the brand name to "Caribe," which was used until 1976.

The plate shown was made under the "Caribe" name in 1961, an unusual addition to the 1960s Western ware, with its 1940s feel of hats, spurs, and brands.

The main Sterling plant in Wellsville continues to this day, manufacturing medium-gauge vitrified china for commercial use. Decals are designed and produced in-house, and a full gamut of decorative application is used, from custom transfer prints and decals to a variety of glazes and surface decorations.

Right: Russel Wright design for Sterling China for Harold's Club Casino, the first modern casino in Reno, Nevada, that opened in 1941. An Old West theme defined the interior with a world-class gun collection and an outdoor wagon train mural (still preserved at the Reno Livestock Events Center). In 1979 Harold's was sold to Howard Hughes. The establishment folded in 1999.
Top right: Dinner plate by Sterling with Old West border well worn. A real survivor.

The 1970s

For a generation of Baby Boomers, the 1970s marked a coming of age. The innocence of childhood in the post war '50s and the psychedelic '60s was tarnished by the realities of an escalating Vietnam war. The United States armed forces were drawn increasingly into battle until the taking of Saigon and the end of America's involvement in 1975. In protest, the anti-war movement defined a decade, with carnage at Kent State and protestors advocating a revolt against government and big business.

Watergate ushered out Richard Nixon, and Gerald Ford took his place. Women's lib took to the streets and contraceptive clinics opened their doors, while the environmental movement found an early voice in the words and voice of eco-evangelist singer/songwriter John Denver.

The Carnaby Street look took over fashion—mini skirts, platform shoes, and bell bottom pants. At the same time, the film *Saturday Night Fever* fueled the heat of a younger generation. The term polyester double knit became a household word.

Mainstream television programming favored shows with a social conscience, like *All In the Family,* and the once-favorite TV Westerns like *The Virginian, Bonanza,*

Tin coffee cups with decals of Cartwright brothers from *Bonanza* (not vintage).

and *Gunsmoke* finally ended their runs. The Western and all its familiar faces were history. Jimmy Carter was voted into the White House, and Iran was his Waterloo.

The film world passed on Westerns in favor of science fiction and space cowboys. Luke Skywalker rode into the frontiers of the galaxy in *Star Wars*. A smoother, more sophisticated hero catered to adult fantasies when Roger Moore and Sean Connery starred as Agents 007. Toward the end of the '70s, jarring films about the Vietnam war brought home the message of the price we paid.

As 1980 approached, America got an unexpected dose of boots and denim with John Travolta in *Urban Cowboy*. The Western craze caught on in the mainstream, and suddenly being a cowboy was hip again. Sales in denim doubled, and cowboy boots came back into mainstream style.

Stillmeadow Pottery

1970–Current

Founder of Stillmeadow Pottery, Jim Ralph of El Dorado, California, likes to think of himself as the manufacturer who held it all together during the Dark Ages of Western dinnerware—from 1970 to 1990. In fact, he believes he helped usher in the revival.

"Back in the 1970s," said Ralph, "I was a self-taught potter and decided to develop my passion into a business. I started with the intention of making turn-of-the-century ware, including crocks and churns, to be a part of the trend in Americana. But with an ongoing interest in the Western lifestyles, I explored the Country

Oval platter by Charley Van Troba for Stillmeadow Pottery. Branding in the traditional manner.

genre further and evolved my designs and products into the Western and Lodge collections, which fortunately found a market. As the business grew, we expanded our operation to keep up with the demand both here in the U.S. and in many foreign countries."

Jim also took Stillmeadow directly to the customer by selling at rodeos and fairs throughout the West. He offered the option of putting the customer's brand on the dinnerware along with images of their choice, and they loved it.

"My main goal was to customize and personalize. Either for an individual, club, or restaurant, we could design for them. At the time, no one was doing that. I learned early on that people had to make a connection with the ware. If they walked into my booth and I could personalize the dinnerware for them, they'd make the purchase. A functional family heirloom could be created that hopefully would be passed down through generations."

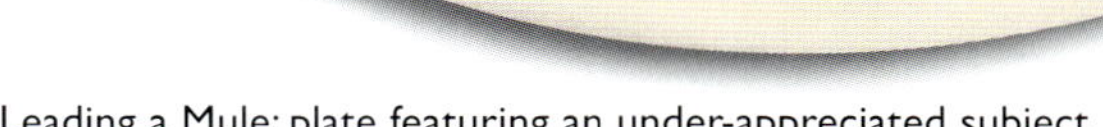

Leading a Mule: plate featuring an under-appreciated subject.

More tableware designed by Charley Van Troba for Stillmeadow Pottery. Horse head, bronco, and chuck wagon are exemplary.

In time, Ralph discovered which designs sold in different regions. For example, team roping is a huge sport in Texas, so he commissioned his artists to draw team ropers. Likewise with Hereford cattle and mules—animals

Examples of the licensed dinnerware made for the Roy Rogers and Dale Evans Museum gift store in Victorville, California, in the 1970s by Stillmeadow Pottery. Line drawings based on archival photos.

that are important to many, but rarely seen on dinnerware. He offered over one hundred images in several glaze colors that could be applied on a white or tan heavy porcelain body to create the buyer's own personal look.

What had been most appealing about the dinnerware was the wide range of line drawings by artists Lynn Brown and Charley Van Troba of Nevada. Stillmeadow made its own decals of these images using the on-glaze decal method, which melts permanently onto the surface of the ware.

"In the 1990s, the Roy Rogers Museum called and asked me to develop a line of ware with Roy's images," Ralph said. "I spent three days going through the museum's archives and pulled out pictures that would translate into workable drawings. The line has since become a part of the world of Roy Rogers collectibles."

Also at that time, Ralph's pottery found its way into the prop inventory for a film called *The Edge,* staring Anthony Hopkins and Alec Baldwin, filmed in the Northwest in a hunting lodge. Stillmeadow was just what they were looking for.

Ralph recently sold the business to Marsha Roth, a rancher in northern California who loves the company and intends to keep it going, catering to the individual, club, restaurant, or retailer who sees the obvious advantage of a customized product.

Charley Van Troba

Charley Van Troba has lived the life he creates, inspired by the long standing traditions of the Buckaroo way—cattle ranching and horsemanship as perfected in the Spanish heritage, with its emphasis on artistry, skill, and style. He's worked on ranches and gathered cattle on a spread as large as four million acres out in Nevada, working a herd of 10,000–12,000. That's a hard ride, in the saddle all day.

He has been making images for dinnerware decals for Stillmeadow ever since meeting Jim Ralph in 2003 at Cowboy Christmas in Las Vegas, where he shows his originals and prints to an appreciative audience. Not that he isn't well known in his own area—he's been a frequent entry to the Winnemucca Buckaroo Heritage Art Show and has received the Will James Award nine years in a row. "In fact," says Van Troba, "there's an eerie connection between Will James and myself. James died on February 20, 1942, and I was born on the same day."

A ranch horse by an artist who knows how to handle a pencil. (Courtesy Buckaroo Heritage Art Show, Nevada)

At home in Kingston, two hundred miles east of Reno, he loves the cowboy life. "We're 136 miles from the nearest grocery store," he said, but would not have it any other way.

Van Troba enjoys capturing his cowboy subjects in oil, pen and ink, pencil, and watercolor. Subjects include cowboys with wooly chaps on broncos, portraits of Longhorns and mustangs, and newborn colts resting on the ground.

Van Troba shows annually at the Cowboy Poetry Gathering in Elko, and until recently, sold only originals. Now, offset prints make his work available to more admirers. He sends new drawings to Stillmeadow Pottery once a year and they plan new releases around them.

The 1980s

The 1980s saw the collapse of communism in eastern Europe and an increase in violence in the Middle East. America's wealth and production began to move to newly industrialized countries, changing the world order. Ronald Reagan presided as the Cold War came to an end.

It was a time of greed and the "Me" generation, of Cable TV, the music video, and a stock market crash of major proportions. John Lennon was murdered in 1980, and Michael Jackson emerged to win over American audiences with *Thriller,* a record-breaking album.

Fashion brought shoulder pads to women's wear. Power dressing accompanied the climb up the corporate ladder in pantsuits. Rising star/designer Ralph Lauren invigorated American fashion and introduced the feel of the West as a shared American heritage. Prairie skirts, Navajo blouses, jeans, and denim jackets were available for urban dudes, all accented with Native American jewelry, cowboy hats, and boots. Denim was mainstream and everybody's wardrobe staple. Jeans weren't just for cowboys anymore. In fact, a legion of teenagers and college students probably never knew they once were.

Television Westerns had been replaced by Texas-based series like *Dallas* and *Dynasty.* J.R. Ewing wore the hat,

Enesco salt shaker with line drawings of cowboys lounging around a chuck wagon fire.

but the horse had clearly been left behind. In film, science fiction still dominated the studios, with *ET* as the top grossing film. Super hero Indiana Jones battled forces in exotic locales and *Batman* made millions. The themes hadn't changed—merely the players. *Silverado,* a Western made in 1985 with Kevin Costner, turned heads with a story about small town justice. The Old West came back with characters bigger than life by Texas author Larry McMurtry, whose epic novel *Lonesome Dove* won a Pulitzer Prize in 1986.

Few china manufacturers were making anything with Western imagery during this time. But like a long lost relative who seemed to disappear, the Western was destined to return again. It was just a matter of time.

Enesco, LLC

1888–Current

Enesco is an international entity that has been in business in the Chicago area since the late 1800s, importing Japanese-made ware to America. The 1950s and '60s were key years in the import of ceramic figures and novelties, especially kitchenware, banks, and planters. Enesco is best known for a highly sought after line of sentimental cast collectibles known as "Precious Moments, which it offered from 1993 to 2005, along with Jim Shore collectible items." The items that I collected reference the jugs of an earlier era with nostalgic chuck

Old-time cowboy camp scene by Enesco in semi-glazed stoneware—it's nice to see someone hasn't forgotten. Some things get better with age.

wagon scene decals and brown glaze accent called "westward Ho." Although Enesco has not been a producer of Western ware per se, it's interesting to note that they brought out a Western-themed group during a time when few were looking for it.

Hartstone Pottery
1980–2005

"Sky Ranch" by Hartstone and Carlisle China. A great concept and a great product, heavy enough to be industrial strength.

Yet another company out of America's twentieth-century past can be credited for a well-designed and authentic Western collection—this one called "Sky Ranch."

The name of the collection is actually the name of the company that first created it, founded in Santa Fe in the 1980s. Sky Ranch was purchased and reissued in the 1990s by a new owner, Brannon Brewer. The talented artist who drew the original artwork was Sam Yeats from Austin, Texas, who had a knack for capturing the vintage look of the Old West in his masterful drawings of a cowboy roping a Longhorn, a buckaroo, a cowgirl on a bronco, a barrel racer, plus various motifs like Longhorn heads, brands, and boots.

Sky Ranch was finally purchased in 1998 by Carlisle Food Service Products and marketed alongside its Hartstone Pottery Company of Zanesville, Ohio. Hartstone was originally founded in 1976 by Pat Hart, and then sold to Carlisle in 1996. Hartstone was dedicated to quality stoneware cooking and baking products as well as dinnerware. Carlisle discontinued the sales of the "Sky Ranch" dinnerware line soon after selling the Hartstone Pottery Company in 2005.

Place settings and accessories were sold as open stock, and were decorated either in red, sepia brown, green, or black glaze on an off-white stoneware body. The pieces are thick and heavy and highly decorative, with wonderful utility items like sugars and creamers. "Sky Ranch" continues to be bought and sold among collectors and is a valued series among all who search for Western-themed china.

The 1990s

The decade of the '90s saw a shift toward a new concern for the environment matched by a new kind of entrepreneurship. Self-styled individuals were shaping a new society in a world of instant communication.

America's streets were filled with fashions from the '60s, while restaurants went global, developing a new national palette that craved sushi, Tex Mex, or Thai food. Television ushered in the era of *Baywatch* and *Seinfeld, The Simpsons* (the first ever adult-targeted cartoon show) and *Sex in the City*. Although the classic law-and-order Western had faded, a last attempt at the TV Western serial came about with *Dr. Quinn Medicine Woman*, a series about a female doctor in a small Western town, a familiar formula with a new spin that enjoyed smash ratings.

America tasted terrorism at home in 1995 with the Oklahoma City bombing, an unthinkable event. At our nation's capital, a president disgraced his office in a relationship with an intern. In Colorado, the Columbine Massacre shocked a nation and spurred debates on gun control.

Longhorn motif fruit or cereal bowl by Buckeye Blake, "Cow Camp" china, for Pipestone.

Western Movies

In the '90s, Epic Westerns, Romantic Westerns, and even "Acid" Westerns (*The Deadman* with Johnny Depp) competed with traditional Westerns like Tom Selleck's *Quigley Down Under, Young Guns,* and the widely acclaimed *Conagher* with Sam Elliot. The comedic *City Slickers* made us see the Western in a whole new light. So did Brad Pitt's *Legends of the Fall.*

Clint Eastwood gave us *Unforgiven*, and Ed Harris was memorable in *Riders of the Purple Sage.* A made for television movie, *You Know My Name,* brought Sam Elliot back in a classic lawman role. He showed up as the cowboy in *The Big Lebowski,* a comedy, in 1998 as well. *The Horse Whisperer* gave us the ultimate message—that the West can heal the most damaged of individuals, horses included.

In short, moviegoers could have their Westerns whenever they wanted them. The younger set would have to settle for video game versions of good guys versus bad guys, or tune in to the Westerns Channel to watch *Lone Ranger* reruns just as they were seen in the '50s. A creation of Starz Encore Media, the debut of this specialty station on cable television in 1994 gave everyone who missed the old days a chance to relive them with Western serials and films.

Hollywood had a new crop of directors and producers who actually managed to deliver some of the finest traditional and revisionist Westerns to date, like *Tombstone* and *Dances With Wolves.* But they were desperate to reinvent Westerns to sell to new markets, which caused viewers to suffer Science Fiction Westerns like *Wild Wild West* with Kevin Kline, Horror Westerns like the *Quick and the Dead* with Sharon Stone, and even Vampire Westerns such as *Sundown: The Vampire in Retreat* with David Carradine.

Country music was on the rise and crossover cowboy/country star George Strait made being a cowboy seem very cool. The rest of the world continued to come West in droves, to be enriched by our mountains, our prairies, and our sunsets.

According to Jane and Michael Stern's epic biography, *Happy Trails, Our Life Story,* the story of Dale Evans and Roy Rogers, "By 1990, it seemed that Americans were once again eager to embrace the West … BMW's were traded in on pickup trucks, Rolexes gave way to Wranglers, and cowboy boots appeared on feet once shod by Gucci. Cowboy cool had gained even more momentum in the '90s as an antidote to the rampant sleaze of pop-cultural hypocrisy of so many public figures in politics. … Consider America's cowboy hero—you'll never see him ranting about his problems to Oprah or Geraldo (Rivera) … nor filling out a medical insurance claim form. In the movie West of Hollywood's imagination, there are no corporate committees to decide when to saddle up … and little in the way of meddling government to obstruct a buckaroo with a job to do."

Whether the returning re-emphasis on the West was an alternative to the harried frenzy of big city living, a return to American values, or a fantasy realized, it was making itself felt on the home front, in fashion, and on the table.

Pipestone

1976–Current

One of the first manufacturers to bring the cowboy back to the dining room, Pipestone created one of the most collectible sets ever sold at retail. Along with artist Buckeye Blake, owner Kathleen Kindig produced the hugely successful "Cow Camp" series in 1990, a collection far ahead of its time.

Mimbreno pattern—Pipestone knew a good thing when they saw it. Keeping this historic collection alive is part of the stewardship needed in protecting great designs.

Kindig has been business since 1976 in Red Lion, Pennsylvania. But her company didn't start there. Originally it was founded as Nostalgia Station, Ltd., the official gift shop of the B&O Railroad Museum in Baltimore, Maryland, and served eight years in that capacity. The shop was well known for carrying all kinds of railroad memorabilia.

"We were dedicated to bringing a sense of history and uniquely American style to the home dining experience," said Kindig. "We still are. We found that we had a real appreciation for the dining car china that made riding the rails such a luxurious experience in America's past. Based on that affinity, Pipestone, a name we chose around 1990 with Buckeye Blake's help, evolved into the quality dinnerware manufacturer we've become today. All our ware is high-fired vitreous china clay, so sturdy it has fused into glass, just like that used on the trains of our nation's most elite railroads. It's durable, microwave and dishwasher safe, and designed to bring dining pleasure for many years to come."

Because Kendig worked at the railroad museum and was already selling railroad china, she was able to secure a license from the Santa Fe Railway (now known as the Burlington Northern and Santa Fe Railway, or BNSF, since their merger in 1996) and began to produce their much-loved historic "Mimbreno" pattern once used on the Santa Fe dining cars.

Pipestone utilizes already-finished china blanks, made by various producers, whose quality meets Kendig's high standards. Then decals are created using commissioned artwork. Each color is a separate glaze, and it goes on much like the art of silk screening, with exacting registers and painstaking placement, all by hand. The technique is called "on glaze" and is essentially a glaze itself, fusing with the top glaze and making a glass-like, smooth surface. Over the years, her company has supplied tableware to some of the finest catalog companies in America, like Horchow and Sundance, reaching a nationwide audience.

Top: "Cow Camp" by Buckeye Blake for Pipestone makes me want to get up and do the two-step. Here the old West meets the new, bold and playful. The many serving pieces (not shown) tell the rest of the story. Superb.
Above: "Prairie Rose," the fairer sex finally got her due. Hats off to Kathy Kendig and Teal Blake.

Current patterns available from Pipestone include the legendary "Mimbreno" pattern, one of their most popular, which is available in black and gray or black and burgundy, on an off-white or ivory plate (also called American white). In the mid-2000s Kendig released "Prairie Rose," with artwork by Teal Blake, a collection featuring the American cowgirl, an idea whose time had come.

"The cowgirl is such a romantic theme," added Kendig. " I wanted to portray her, especially with women everywhere finally coming into their own."

A master of Western skies and everyday subjects, his vision is clear and bold.

Artist Buckeye Blake

Texas artist Buckeye Blake is a master of many mediums, both two- and three-dimensional. A popular fine artist and graphic designer whose posters for various Western events are as collectible as his original paintings, he's also been commissioned to create sculptures immortalizing Western legends like Kit Carson and Charles Russell.

Raised in the cowboy tradition, Buck has first-hand knowledge of ranch life and the challenges of working on the land. "I grew up in the West and came from a family of artists," said Blake. "My dad was also a rodeo cowboy. My father had this old dude ranch dinnerware, probably made in Mexico, with pictures of *vaqueros* on it. I still remember it."

Blake's style rings with authenticity and reflects the tradition of Western art as established by Russell—highly literal and narrative, yet firmly anchored in the present. His strength in design is evident in everything he does. Although he's collected by major museums, he's not afraid to create for more popular mediums, dinnerware among them. The first artist to create a Western pattern for Pipestone, he was asked to limit the design to four colors. Like the rest of Pipestone's durable products, the dinnerware would be made of hotel-grade high-fired vitreous china with a clean white clay body.

"I chose three warm colors and one cool," said Blake, "which gave me a workable balance." The result is a rich mix of reds and blues against the West's all-pervasive brown. The collection, called "Cow Camp," is an absolute celebration of Western life. The various pieces incorporated the most revered symbols of the West, including the bucking bronco, the saddle, the Longhorn and the ranch horse, which are duly bordered by brands or coiled rope. Mugs illustrate chaps or a

campfire, while platters have graphics of a trick roper, a wagon driver, or a cowgirl—hat thrown back, flicking her quirt. Each image is both fresh and deliberate, reflecting the exacting requirements of the transfer process, which requires the separation of colors. "The variety was the evolution of an idea," Blake said. "We wanted to have different images on every piece."

Buck might be a cowboy at heart, but he's a citizen of the world. He's traveled and studied throughout Europe and America, and has been influenced by everyone from the Taos Group to Charles Russell, as well as popular culture. The starry heavens, for example, found on the dinner plate and serving platters in the "Cow Camp" pattern have an unexpected boldness about them, almost a Pop Art reference in their twinkly irregularity. No Western artist ever made the heavens shine quite this way.

Following "Cow Camp" came "Cow Camp Baby," a similar set for children with a two-handled cup and a divided plate, equally attractive. Here, as in his work on canvas, Blake succeeds in a contemporary rendition of traditional Western images. Although these patterns were retired in 2005, rare finds of "Cow Camp" are a collector's dream.

Gaetano Pottery

1806–Current

A variety of producers helped bring the 1990s to life. You might not have heard about this Florida based company, makers of a unique and select series.

Gaetano: Breezy and smart, this sophisticated design was drawn by someone who really knew their cowboy. Simple line art with chili pepper border made this an affordable production and a very effective one.

Above: Lone Ranger by Vandor, a remarkable collectible released in 2003, a limited edition of 4,800 pieces, hand numbered. This fine cookie jar seems to embody the Western movie era. It has enormous presence. (Courtesy Michele Mosko, photo by Lindsay Allen) Right: Cowhide patterned cup with bucking bronco titled "American Frontier," made in Japan for Vandor, 1991. The inside rim sports famous cattle brands.

According to their current media, "Gaetano Pottery was founded in 1806 by Gaetano Miali in Los Angeles, California. The company evolved from a Western and Country–look earthenware ceramics manufacturer to a contemporary housewares line in the '90s. Today they are specialty manufacturers to the hospitality industry."

Retired employee Art Henares adds this: "When Gaetano's new owner, Irving Chait, bought the company in 1986, he was the fourth generation owner, and I was the General Manager of the company. I remember we had a lot of product lines in crocks, mixing bowls, bean pots, and water coolers in different colors—products with blue and brown stripes, hand-painted lines in different designs, such as the "Cowboy," and many more. Then, in 2005, Irving Chait sold the business to Bill Scatchard, whose corporate office is located in Orange City, Florida. The image you see here is an 8.5-inch pasta bowl. We had three sizes of pasta bowls, namely the 8.5-inch, the 12.5-inch and the 15-inch. They were our "Cowboy with Chili" line made in the early 1990s, with a cowboy twirling his rope surrounded by chili peppers."

Vandor
1994–Current

Vandor was founded by one of the pioneers of the American gift industry, Ted Vandorn, in 1957. Since being acquired by Lyon Corporation in 1994, the company has cornered the market in nostalgic licensed dinnerware. Today, Vandor Originals feature some of the hottest properties in the industry—pop culture favorites like John Wayne,® I Love Lucy,® Elvis Presley,® and Betty Boop.™

Rich in heritage, retired Vandor dinnerware is now traded at ever higher values on the Internet and other secondary markets, and it enjoys a loyal following among fans and collectors.

Vandor remains an innovator in the gift and home décor industries. With the philosophy that great products sell themselves, their goal is to provide products that surprise, delight, and entertain. Now based in Salt Lake City, Utah, they have offices in Hong Kong, China, and the Philippines. Although the remarkable cookie jar based on the Lone Ranger and made recently isn't really dinnerware, I couldn't resist including it. A design that's retired, he's a friendly reminder of the glory that was.

The New Millennium

2000–2010

The much anticipated Age of Aquarius that the Woodstock generation so firmly believed in never happened. Instead, we were barely into the new millennium when the world was rocked by the horror of 9/11. Prior to this terrifying event, America was involved with global interdependent trade, a shared world energy crisis (as well as our own in housing and credit), and the rise of climatic shifts and global warming.

The decade was marked by stock market amateurs, the presidency of George W. Bush, and the rise of corporate giants like Walmart. Starbucks spread in our cities, along with much needed urban revitalization. On the streets, retro fashions evoked the 1940s all over again, and a generation of young home owners filled their condos and rehabs with Mid-century Modern and Post-war classics. Fashion was casual and Bohemian, footwear was all about pointed toes, high heels, flat-soled Uggs, and, more than ever—cowboy boots. Heavy Metal reigned, along with Pop, Punk, Hip Hop, and the growing popularity of Country Music, gaining bigger audiences each year.

The West came back in a variety of big screen and made-for-television films, most for export. In fact, the

Pendleton's "Grand Lodge" dinnerware, commemorative plate released in 2009 to celebrate the company's centennial.

bulk of the Westerns made were Manchurian Westerns, Samurai Westerns, and Space Westerns, most of which fortunately were never seen in this country.

The big favorites in this new century were made-for-television movies like *Crossfire Trail* and *Monte Walsh,* both starring Tom Selleck. In 2003, Kevin Costner and Robert Duvall brought us back to the gritty frontier in *Open Range.*

In 2004, *Hidalgo* brought a romantic figure on a horse to the fore, and in 2005, searching for a new kind of audience, *Brokeback Mountain* brought us a relationship/cowboy story that was unexpected in the genre. But behind all the story lines was a suggested return to that sacred landscape that shaped a cowboy's life.

Following the tragedy of 9/11, in fact, an article appeared in the *New York Times* asking people where they felt safest in the event that terror continued to be struck at home. Overwhelmingly, the answer was—out West. Increased retreats to dude ranches and moves to rural Western towns followed. A majority of interviewees felt that terror would never strike in the land of the cowboy. And so they came to the West for comfort and protection, and continue to do so.

It's not so much the low-density population centers or the camouflage of our landscape that draws them, but the fact that the West has become an emotional and physical stronghold, a place where, in some people's mind, evil cannot stand.

It's no wonder that Western-inspired products started to hit the shelves that year. The time was ripe.

Montana Lifestyles
(Montana Silversmiths)
2000–Current

Most regular customers of Western supply and feed stores can remember when a section known as Western Lifestyles didn't exist. After all, placemats, fancy pillows, and shower curtains just weren't what most ranchers were looking for. Denim jeans, Western shirts, and work gloves were.

However, most did expect to find goods bearing the name of Montana Silversmiths, an enterprising manufacturer in Columbus, Montana, that, since 1973, has made extraordinary Western belt buckles, jewelry, saddle trim, and other accessories in plated silver. The company's goal has always been to bring high-quality, low-cost silver-plated goods to the marketplace. Their engraving is decorative and beautiful, and their product well displayed in handsome glass cases coast to coast. To many, Montana Silversmiths is a household word.

In addition, Montana Silversmiths has supported various organizations, from the Professional Rodeo Cowboys Association to the American Quarter Horse Association, and even professional bull riding. One buckle at a time, they slowly grew to establish their credibility with ranchers and horse owners nationwide.

Above: "Iron Star," bold and simple in tobacco and blue. By Montana Lifestyles. (Courtesy Montana Lifestyles)

Today, they're the largest manufacturer of Western silver products in the world, with dealer-partners in all fifty states and in many foreign countries. They also offer custom-made trophy buckles for major Western events and world championships—fine hand-crafted works of art engraved with precision. In the last few years, the company has also applied the art of fine Western design to handbags, wallets, and other leather accessories to compliment their Western silver and to further serve their Western customer.

And they make dinnerware.

Montana Silversmiths' credibility with the consumer paved the way into uncharted territory back in 2000, on the trail of well-designed Western home décor. They saw the success in mainstream retail and were determined to offer their customers a new range of branded

"Branded," the simplicity of the motif lends itself to every shape of this collection.

Montana Lifestyles' latest addition, 2010. "Tooled Leather" dinnerware with embossed raised floral border. So very much in the tradition—leather carving and flowers are near and dear to the heart of Western culture.

"Ironstar"—Montana Lifestyle's early success. This collectible group dressed any table in brilliant blue and rust.

products. During the '90s, home décor was among the fastest-growing retail segments nationwide, expressed by mega-stores like the now defunct Linens n Things or Bed, Bath and Beyond.

Ranch-based customers weren't looking for decorative items with Montana Silversmiths' name on it, but they didn't resist when the trendy new Western Lifestyles sections began to flourish in Western chain stores like Shepler's and Boot Barn.

Montana Silversmiths started their new off-shoot with a line of Western inspired picture frames, candles, holiday ornaments, furniture items, bath décor, and china, all gathered under the heading of Montana Lifestyles. Their very first dinnerware group featured a warm beige leather-look glaze on an earthenware body, enhanced with embossed brands in a rich brown, and a fancy "rope" trim, or edge. A success when it debuted, the collection aptly called "Branded" can be credited with the revival of Western dinnerware practically overnight. After what had been a long absence in the tabletop industry, the genre was back, with a clear choice for the homeowner who wanted to set a table that reflected their Western heritage.

"Belt buckles are the billboards of the West."

—**Judy Wagner,** Marketing Director, Montana Silversmiths

Montana Lifestyles' commitment to the new direction resulted in the production of a new dinnerware group every few years since. Each effort expressed a uniquely different design statement, from the striking effect of "Iron Star" to the horse round-up of "Montana Traditions," to the sentimental illustrations of Paul Cameron Smith, to the very latest carved leather floral border collection.

Norby Studio Ltd.

2002–Current

Far in the north of Wyoming, the Norby Studio Ltd., owned by Thomas and Kim Norby, is turning out some of the most compelling hand-thrown porcelain pottery in the country. The couple began their studio-based business back in 1985, at home in Montana in the Gallatin Valley. In 2002, they moved to Black Hills country, not far from Sundance, Wyoming. Wherever they've lived, nature has surrounded them and has always been their inspiration.

Artist Thomas has a rare talent for capturing the very essence of wildlife. In his work, eagles soar, bears lumber, and elk saunter around the curves and planes of their

Top: Thomas and Kim Norby (photo by Norbys).
Left: Norby original handmade airbrushed platter.
Right: Imported "Montana Traditions" collection dinner plate in sepia glaze.

bowls, pitchers, and plates. His technique is classic airbrush over stencil, an application that seems flat in the hands of lesser artists, but in his case manages to create a full sense of three-dimension, in part due to his ability to dissolve colors and shapes into mist.

Both artists attended the University of Montana, where they met in the ceramics department. Thom graduated in 1975 with a BFA in painting, but he's also adept at stone sculpture. Kim focused on drawing and the technique of wheel-thrown clay. A native of Rapid City, South Dakota, she is most influenced by Scandinavian designs, her love for the Black Hills, and arctic landscapes.

While living in Montana, the couple made frequent trips to Yellowstone Park to photograph the vast herds of elk and bison, along with grizzlies, black bears, and wolves. Around their studio, now located in canyon country, are whitetail and mule deer, elk, and mountain lions. Kim and Thom frequently visit their cabin, located in the Norbeck Wildlife Preserve in the heart of South Dakota's Black Hills, to hike and watch wildlife.

The lead-free porcelain that comprises their work is hand-thrown on a potter's wheel by Kim and individually glazed by Thom. No two pieces are exactly alike. They are fired to over 2,300 degrees F., are safe for use with all foods, and can be used in an oven, microwave, and dishwasher.

"Montana Traditions," a commission created for Montana Lifestyles back in 2002, was their first and only design for the manufacturer. Translated into sepia and brown on an off-white clay body that was produced offshore, the image depicts a wild horse roundup. The original concept is an astonishing piece of art. You can literally feel the horse jerk as the rope settles around his neck. A true Western moment, this plate seems suitable for framing.

Hand-thrown water pitcher by Norbys; creamer by Montana Lifestyles.

For the sake of comparison, both the original and the mass-produced versions of the plate and two different types of pitchers are shown here. Other accessory pieces to the line are equally successful. With luck, the dinnerware world may one day see more of their work.

Montana Lifestyles Continues

Dinnerware with cowgirls and old time bronc busters—feels like vintage dinnerware but with a new twist.

"Boots" was the next collection created by Montana Lifestyles, reminiscent of the famed McCoy pottery of the 1950s with its relief (raised) imagery, lightly glazed for accent. The look mimics carved stone just as effectively as its famed predesessor.

"Boots" by Montana Lifestyles. Reminiscent of Nelson McCoy ware. (Courtesy Montana Lifestyles)

Next came the "Vintage Ranch" collection with the nostalgic art by Texas artist Lynn Brown. Each piece is created in the spirit of the cowgirl or the working cowboy and reinforces the classic feel of the Old West. Lynn's style in watercolor, translated to a decal, is diffused and soft and feels like a hand-colored photograph.

Lynn Brown's designs make stoneware table settings endearing, a rare quality to find in a mass-produced product. Her designs for Montana Lifestyles wed the West of yesterday to today, utilizing photographic transfers that capture her original artworks precisely, down to their soft edges and diffused imagery. The result is almost like looking through the lens of time into the characters of a century ago.

Lynn Brown. Is it fair to say this pretty cowgirl looks like one of her paintings? (Courtesy Lynn Brown, photo by Stan Brown)

When asked if the cowgirls in the "Vintage Ranch" collection, who seem so real, are modeled after actual or living subjects, Lynn replied, "I look for images, faces, and incorporate them into the cowgirls from all sources. I'm often inspired by old photos from 1910 through 1940. With these women, I try to capture their grit and beauty and show them in a respectful attitude. They established a place for themselves in the early world of rodeo with their own skill and tenacity, while taking the practical clothing of the cowboy and applying lace, beads, fringe, and bows and making a style all their own. It's what makes them still admired today."

"Champion" by Lynn Brown. A cowgirl who knows who she is. (Courtesy Tom Alexia photography)

Lynn was born in Texas and raised in Arizona, where she was exposed to horses and ranching and developed a deep love for the lifestyle. Now, back in Texas in Bluffdale, near Fort Worth, she's committed full time to her art. Her watercolors and oils have been exhibited in many shows throughout the West, including the Trappings of the American West in Arizona, and the Phippen Miniature Art Show. Her work has been chosen to represent the Santa Clarita Cowboy

Poetry and Music Festival and numerous other festivals and gatherings. Her highly skilled renderings of horses, cowboys, rodeo broncs, and other western characters feel familiar, yet new. Her style is a sharp contrast to the glossy hard surface of vitreous china, but the contrast works to great advantage.

Montana Lifestyles surrounds the central design with burnt orange edges, reminiscent of restaurant china from the 1940s and '50s with their brown and orange airbrushed accents. Everything about the pattern evokes a vintage feel. Lynn's larger portfolio encompasses the everyday world of ranch work, as well.

"I especially enjoy trying to capture the day-to-day life of the working cowboy and the horse, said Lynn. "When I smell the summer rains that wash everything clean again, see a cow with a newborn calf, or an early winter snow, I'm inspired to paint this way of life. I believe that art should bring pleasure to the viewer, capture a moment in time. Scenes and scenery change, people change, times change, but art can hold you there always, as you remember it or wish to."

Lynn is a traditional artist as well, with a very painterly approach. (Courtesy Tom Alexander Photography, Flagstaff, Arizona)

Paul Cameron Smith

Branded Dinnerware for Montana Lifestyles

The most recent release of dinnerware by Montana Lifestyles (2009) is the new group called "Paul Cameron Smith Branded Dinnerware." This artist's traditional images of the cowboy make every plate a work of art. The detail and mood of his designs evokes the early years of the traditional illustrators who gave us the standard by which all dinnerware seems to be compared.

Paul Cameron Smith collection: a table setting that tells a human story at every individual place setting. (Courtesy Montana Lifestyles)

Texas artist Paul Cameron Smith brings a fresh view of the West with his timeless collection of images. One design among the four includes a cowboy fixing fence with his young son. Yet another depicts a cowboy about to receive a kiss from his sweetheart while astride his horse, and yet another shows a young cowpoke about to mount up on his patient ranch pony—all glimpses of a special moment in everyday ranch life.

The brown and cream-colored dinnerware collection has a casual but elegant feel, with a wide cocoa-brown border with incised brands carved into the surface. The center of the plates features a monochromatic image drawn originally with remarkable detail. This current collection might be Montana Silversmith's most successful presentation to date—strong, yet deeply sentimental.

Top: (Photo by Paul Cameron Smith)
Above: Nothing is lost in the translation from paper to dinnerware. "Learnin to Rope," another perfect moment in ranch life.

Smith is a consummate draftsman, at ease with pen and ink or pencil. "With the release of my first pencil drawing print in 1991," explains Smith, "titled 'One for the Road,' I found an immediate market for my Western-themed art. This first series of five hundred prints sold out in nine months and gave me the confidence I needed to pursue a career as a full-time artist. In the next several years, I continued to release an average of two to three prints per year. These sold well enough to work full time at my new passion. In the past eighteen years, I've released over sixty-five prints and have sold my art all over the U.S. and overseas as well."

In 2003, while attending the Cowboy Christmas Gift Show in Las Vegas, Paul was approached by a marketing director for Montana Silversmiths, who was seeking a new artist that they could feature for their Western-themed products. An agreement was quickly established, and a series of collector watch boxes featuring his art was released thereafter.

"As a result of this product release," continued Smith, "I was asked by Montana Silversmiths if I would be interested in having a series of

"We believe that tableware is the ultimate in reflecting "Western Lifestyle" as it relates to your décor, taste, passion, and lifestyle. Western-themed tabletop sets the stage for family and friends, serving as conversation pieces and as a backdrop for memories that will be treasured for a lifetime."
—**Dennis Potzman,** former President and CEO, Montana Silversmiths

"Ladies First," "Cherished," "Courting Cowboy," and "Daddy's Hands" proving there's more to ranching than cows. (Courtesy Montana Lifestyles)

sculptures produced that were based on my pencil drawings. I was thrilled at the opportunity, and collaborated with them to produce over a dozen resin sculptures labeled the "Paul Cameron Smith Sculpture Series," which was highly successful. In an attempt to further explore the marketability of my images, Montana Silversmiths suggested that they produce a dinnerware set featuring four of my pencil drawings. Once again, I felt this would be a welcome addition to the Paul Cameron Smith brand product realm. The dinnerware has had great initial success. I am thrilled that my art is being featured by such a nationally well-known marketing company and look forward to working with them in the future."

Like many artists, Smith has been attracted to the romance of the West. The wide open spaces and the simple country lifestyle have always appealed to him. "As a young boy of five years, I remember visiting Texas for the first time. It was then that I began to visualize the art that I am producing today. I've thoroughly enjoyed creating each piece of art, and look forward to each new drawing. I thank God each time I sell my work. I'm fortunate to draw for a living, and thank all of you who are interested in my world as I see it and translate it onto paper."

Top: Hay truck with ranch dog. Is this the cutest cookie jar or what? (Courtesy Montana Lifestyles)
Bottom: Elmer, the ultimate cookie jar, just one of many home décor items sporting this whimsical Montana original.

Cowboy Living

2001–Current

Cowboy Living came onto the scene in 2001 and established a signature collection of exemplary tableware in a remarkably short time. Owners Heather and Marty Roberts created a handsome line of beautifully packaged and displayed restaurant-quality dinnerware, available directly to the consumer through their website and select major Western retailers.

The response to their initial effort was positive from the onset, and sales have continued to climb. It's hard to imagine that the former entrepreneur and visionary Heather Roberts, a Seattle-born cowgirl and one-time fashion designer-to-the-stars, and her husband, Marty, once an attorney and professional bull rider, could create a virtual Western dinnerware empire almost overnight, but their vision was huge and their motivation high. Today, the company provides a wide array of decorative and utilitarian items for the table, the entire kitchen, and the bath, presented in a gallery setting with handsome in-store props.

Top: Cowboy Living, cardboard label showing Cowboy Living's logo.
Above: Heather, Lila, Loren, and Marty. (Courtesy Cowboy Living)

"Classic West"—this ranch table setting invites you to stay and linger and enjoy the meal.

Headquartered in Utah, Cowboy Living is best known for producing quality place settings, serving pieces, and oven-to-table bakeware. In less than a decade, they have gained international appeal and celebrity status, notably as the provider of the official dinnerware service of RFD-TV's weekend Western cooking show, *Cowboy Flavor*, seasons one through four.

The company runs as a family effort. "We keep practically everything in-house," said Heather, "which allows

Top: Watercolors by Eve Armson for Cowboy Living proves she's a facile artist with a great feel for the West.
Bottom: Cowboy Living "Barbwire," "Buckaroo," and "Classic West" collections: the sheer diversity of ware makes this the Mother Lode of lines. Circa 2005.

"Buckaroo" stoneware by Cowboy Living: a bold silhouette against a beige background. Stylish Western to mix and match.

us to keep our prices low. We do our own product development and design, most of the photography, and the design and layout of our packaging, plus our own advertising, website, and catalog."

The concept began back in 2001 when Marty and Heather were walking the corridors of retail show Cowboy Christmas in Las Vegas, Nevada. (Marty's father, Monty Roberts, a well-known horse trainer and clinician, had a booth there.)

"While shopping at the Western gift show," said Heather, "we realized that when it came to western dinnerware there just wasn't anything appealing—nothing with a vintage feel that was strong and durable and affordable. We decided to create it ourselves."

Cowboy Living also includes a specialty linen line with embroidery and screen printing, plus coordinating glassware, flatware, and cutlery, as well as platters, metal plate chargers and trays, handsome mugs, serving bowls, serving accessories, and gifts. A chuck wagon cookbook is on the way.

Heather and Marty both had horses while growing up, and they had a feel for and a love of the Old West. The look they were after was "old-fashioned cowboy," evoking authentic ironstone dinnerware from 1930s ranch life. "We wanted our dinnerware to have the look and feel of the vintage dishes we had been collecting, as if the piece had been around forever," explained Marty. "But we also wanted to enrich that with a contemporary feel, layering textures and combining colors."

Heather's mother, Eve Armson, is an artist and paints most of their design ideas. Marty's mom, Pat Roberts, is a sculptress who contributes her talent as well. Former Western film and television star Buck Taylor, a recognized and highly collected watercolor artist in Texas, has contributed several new images for the company since 2007. In particular, a scene of a lawman on an old Western street ("Cowboy Justice") feels wonderfully vintage, as does his next entry, a Longhorn round-up. Between them, all the decorations are originals. The Cowboy Living palette repeatedly uses naturals and neutrals, plus

Every single part of the dining experience has been thought through, from cookware to chargers to napkins to utensils to accessories. (Courtesy Cowboy Living)

shades of cream, beige, and brown, which, according to Heather, customers seem to prefer.

"It's easy to combine pieces from our 'Classic West,' 'Buckaroo,' 'Barbwire,' and "Western Belt" collections," said Heather. "Our varied customers range from city slickers to real ranch folk, and somehow they all connect through our dinnerware."

Connection is precisely the benefit one gets from using this engaging product line. Every table becomes just a little bit Western.

Top: Cowboy Living's "Stampede" platter with watercolor image by Buck Taylor.
Bottom: "Western Belt" pattern nesting bowls. This pattern is also available in the lighter buttercream base color.

Buck Taylor
for Cowboy Living

The name Buck Taylor is familiar to a nation of Baby Boomers who grew up in the glow of the television Western. Entire families gathered together to watch serials like *Gunsmoke* and *Rawhide,* two of the longest running and most memorable series ever produced. Hollywood created great leading roles that were larger than life during that heyday of Western programming, yet the many character actors who helped bring the scripts to life were often just as popular as the leads. One of those was Newly O'Brian on *Gunsmoke,* portrayed by Taylor, who added a kind of endearing charm to the set.

Buck Taylor—An artist and an actor, one of America's film favorites. (Courtesy Buck Taylor)

Still making films today, Taylor looks back on more than fifty years in the business with pride. "The three projects that were my personal favorites," said Taylor, "are *Gunsmoke*, *Gettysburg* (the TV serial), and the film *Tombstone,* where I played the role of Turkey Creek Jack Johnson."

A rancher and real-life cowboy who makes his home in Texas, Buck enjoys team roping and still competes, proving that ranch life can keep a man young. In addition to his skills as a working cowboy, however, he's also a highly accomplished artist in the medium of watercolor, one of the most difficult to master.

"I studied art at the Chouinard Art Institute in Los Angeles before my film career began," said Taylor, "and then basically ignored it for almost thirty years. But around the age of fifty, I felt compelled to get back to my first love—painting in watercolor."

Taylor's favorite subjects are scenes from the Old West. His work is both literal in content and contemporary in approach. Figures are expressive and individualized, and horses, tack, gear, and landscapes are accurate and specific. Yet the artist's brushwork is free and vibrant, and his compositions sparkling and fresh, never overdone. His favorite palette is based on four fundamental colors: alizarin crimson, cadmium yellow, French ultramarine, and burnt sienna. Together, they can express a Western scene that's alive with color, tempered by the burnished feel of the Western landscape. Taylor's images have a definitive romance about them, and his facile brush and keen eye render paintings that sell to discerning collectors of Western art nationwide.

A popular guest at film festivals, rodeos, and state fairs, Taylor has also been honored as the official poster

"Frontier Justice," an original watercolor by Buck Taylor used by Cowboy Living. A great painting and an even more exciting dinnerware design. (Image courtesy Buck Taylor)

"Frontier Justice," by Buck Taylor for Cowboy Living, captures a dramatic moment—a steak platter to frame. (Courtesy Cowboy Living)

artist for the Pendleton Round-Up for the past eleven years. His business manager and helpmate (as well as life soul mate) is his wife Goldie, an accomplished horsewoman and pro barrel racer, ever by his side.

Taylor's private commissions can be found in numerous collections like the Franklin Mint, the American Quarter Horse Museum, and the National Ranching Heritage Museum, to name a few, and private collectors include Sam Elliott, James Arness, Roy Clark, and Val Kilmer, among many others. Thanks to Heather and Marty Roberts, owners of Cowboy Living dinnerware, his remarkable talent can now be enjoyed by the rest of us on our dining tables, as well.

Marty and Heather Roberts were searching for an artist who was firmly anchored in the past, with work that resonated with their vintage-styled product. Malcom Forbes once referred to Taylor as the modern day Remington, a complement well deserved. The Roberts found just what they were looking for in Taylor's "Frontier Justice," a painting inspired by the film *Tombstone,* where the hats that the lawmen wore bore the inscription "Justice is Coming." Applied to their dinnerware, the intriguing combination is a sensation, suitable for display.

"From time to time, I send Heather and Marty new work," said Taylor. "When they find something they like, they know it. Personally, I love the fact that my paintings are shown on a dinner plate. It's actually a functional gift item, not just something you look at on the wall."

For the Western china connoisseur, a new collectible has emerged. "Frontier Justice" is not only a compelling image, well adapted to functional use, but a sign that Western dinnerware has come full circle in offering a narrative illustration. A new means of storytelling has been born to keep the Old West alive.

WesternWare Goods
2004–Current

Leave it to a woman to come West, find love, a new home, discover the photography of a groundbreaking nineteenth-century photographer, and create a new company based on his work. But Abigail Hornik-Minckler isn't just any kind of woman. She's got an extra dose of imagination and guts.

Abigail is a natural entrepreneur who realized a dream of creating high-end products with historic relevance. She conceived the dinnerware line "WesternWare" and traveled overseas in search of a producer who could make it happen with the best materials she could find.

Tipi Platter, photo by L.A. Huffman. Photography and ceramic ware seem made for each other in this attractive platter. (Photo courtesy Western Ware)

Abigail Minckler with Indigo Moon, her Spanish mustang.

Then she proceeded to design a series of irresistible coordinating accessories like lamps and pillows to complement the line.

An ex-New Yorker with a big heart, this high-energy designer is also a compassionate advocate for the voiceless and the disadvantaged. The recipients of her warm-hearted generosity are Montana's wild horses. She's a devoted advocate to their cause, helping them to continue to roam our Western lands.

A horsewoman herself, Abigail understands life in the West and fits in like a native. Ever on the move, she's the design force, the marketing genius, and the vision behind this beautiful and collectible line that appeals to consumers everywhere.

In five short years, she's managed to reintroduce the brilliance of one of America's greatest photographers, L.A. Huffman, to a new generation of photo collectors, interior designers, second-home owners, and history buffs.

Above: Sepia photos, snack server. "Mrs. White Elk," Laton Huffman photo. (Courtesy WesternWare)
Top Right: "Saddling the Wild Horse," photo by Laton Huffman. (Courtesy WesternWare)
Right: Hors D'Oeuvres server: "Cheyenne Plenty Bird in his Sweat Lodge" and other Cheyenne images, Laton Huffman photos. (Courtesy WesternWare)

Few photographers have succeeded in creating such telling portraits of Indians or taken such truthful images of the working cowboy in the early part of the twentieth century.

In her own words, Abigail explains:

"My husband, Thomas Minckler, a third-generation Montanan, turned me on to the magnificent history of the West. I was a native New Yorker at the time, and he was a well-known art dealer for over thirty years, specializing in vintage photography, nineteenth- and twentieth-century Western paintings, rare books, and ephemera. We fell in love and proceeded to split our time between his home in the West and mine in New York City. My design sensibility comes from the urbane environment of the city. The inspiration comes from our passion for the history of the West and our desire to share it with others.

"WesternWare" is designed for peo-

Top left: Place setting by WesternWare: dinner plate, soup bowl ("Mexican John"), salad plate "Round-Up Cook & Pie Biter at Work," plus cup. A one-of-a-kind presentation.
Top right: close-up of salad plate.
Above: 19-inch oval platter "Montana Bedrolls, Pumpkin Creek," Laton Huffman photography.

Erica Hash, owner of Kibler & Kirch, a home décor store in Red Lodge Montana, says this: "'WesternWare' is a good seller here. L.A. Huffman was from this area, and the collection is classy, not so kitschy. Consumers love the smaller groups especially—they make great house gifts. Entire sets of dinnerware sell, as well as the big platters. We love them because they're both historical and Western. Personally, I own a vintage set of 'Winchester 73,' an heirloom from my husband's grandmother. I know how things appreciate."

ple everywhere who love the Western lifestyle and want to integrate their passion into their homes and on their dining table. All the photography that I use for "WesternWare" comes from our personal collections of photos that date from 1886 to 1904."

"WesternWare" was founded officially in 2004. The collection is comprised of high-quality new bone china, with photo decals fused onto the form under a protective top glaze. The colors are true to the original images. Each photo is carefully chosen to complement the surface it will adorn, or in some cases a specific product is made in a mold designed to best accommodate the image. All are suitable for everyday use and are microwave and dishwasher safe. The bold platters and generous plates make great wall décor, and the various sepia photos that adorn smaller dishes are conversation pieces in and of themselves. A replica of L.A. Huffman's signature, along with the date and title of the photo are on the reverse side of the dish. For detailed identification of each item shown, go to www.westernware.net.

WesternWare platter, vase, and place settings. It's easy to set a beautiful table.

About the Photographer

Laton Alton Huffman (1854–1931) is perhaps the most significant photographer of the Old West. During his fifty-year career, he documented the spirit and culture of the Western frontier. He carried his cameras on horseback and shot most of his photos out on the open range. In 1879, he became post photographer at Fort Keogh, Montana Territory, just two years after Custer's battle at Little Big Horn. His camera captured the cowboy and Indian culture, the buffalo herds, and the burgeoning cattle and sheep industry. Both Charlie Russell and Frederic Remington painted from his photographs. His legacy provides us with life portraiture of the northern plains and the pioneering aspects of the area: ranch life, wildlife, frontier town views, and the majestic beauty of Yellowstone National Park.

Laton Huffman. (Courtesy Western Ware)

Timeless Giftware

2004–Current

Partnerships are often a special fusion of talent and organization where new products are born. Timeless Giftware is exactly that, the result of Canadian partners Wayne Tardif on the business end, and artist Bernie Brown on the other. They had a hunch in 2004 that applying Brown's fine art to functional dinnerware would sell, and the results have proven more than correct.

"We thought about a way to turn my artwork into something useful," said Brown, and so the plunge into tableware.

Elegant is the best word that describes the power of black and white china. (Collection courtesy Timeless Giftware)

Brown is a self-taught pencil artist born and raised in Saskatchewan, Canada, whose black and white prints currently sell in over two hundred galleries across North America. His fine original drawings are sold almost before he finishes them, and since they are extremely time consuming, requiring up to one hundred hours each, he rarely creates more than a few new ones per year. His prints, ranging in size from 8 x 11 up through 24 x 30 and created as affordable limited edition offset lithography, are made the same size as his originals, and lack nothing in the translation. The popular prints have been the avenue by which collectors everywhere can enjoy owning his work.

Bernie Brown. (Courtesy Marg Brown)

Distinctively crisp and highly detailed, Brown's drawings remind one of an etching, or even traditional New England scrimshaw, an art form that depends on fine incised lines. The transfer of the original drawings to highly glazed vitreous china is a perfect match of message and material.

Brown left a teaching career in physical education in 1989 to become a full-time artist. At home near Okotoks, Alberta, he and his family now live on a former cattle ranch that's home to fourteen riding horses and a team of Belgians. Bernie devotes his time to drawing and managing the print production and distribution. In addition, he and his wife Margaret own two art galleries in the area.

For the most part, Brown chooses to work in pencil, but adds watercolor occasionally to accent some of his work. His subject matter varies from wildlife to ranch, rodeo, farm, and prairie scenes, each composition a faithful depiction. His style borders on super realism, warmed by a true regard and appreciation for the subject and often with an unexpected touch of sentiment. Puppies lolling on a roping saddle lying on the ground is a good example.

As a horseman and rancher, Brown's rendering of equines, tack, and gear is remarkably precise. That's due in part to working from photographs and real settings.

In fact, all the human characters in his artwork are real persons. The rest is due to his obvious skill. Moreover, the strong compositions lend themselves to the geometry and planes of the china surfaces, which, unlike other collections, come in varying shapes—some round, some square with clipped corners. There's no attempt to rely on any gimmicks or well-worn decorative tricks in any way to make his tableware "Western." In fact, the vibrant dramatic flair of black on white makes these place settings the first elegant, if not dressy, china entries in the Western genre, almost contemporary with plenty of impact.

Each series of images is actually a retired series in the print collection—that is, something

Top: It's remarkable how an image can suit its frame. (Courtesy Timeless Giftware)
Left: A touch of whimsy and puppy love go a long way. (Courtesy Timeless Giftware)

"Young and Restless." At first glance, this fine line drawing almost looks like scrimshaw. Flawless draftsmanship. (Drawing courtesy Timeless Giftware)

Horses seem to be everyone's favorite Western image. (Plate courtesy Timeless Giftware)

he's sold out of on paper. Tardif and Brown collaborate on the choices that define the growing collection, the variety reflecting a wide range of interest.

Brown's original works have been shown at the Charlie Russell Show in Great Falls, Montana, and the Calgary Stampede Western Art Show. They have won numerous national and international print awards. He's taken "Best of Show" at the Calgary Stampede, and was chosen as the Feature Artist for the Calgary Stampede in 2000.

As various editions are added and dropped, Timeless Giftware will become highly collectible, if it isn't already.

Pipestone China
2005–Current

When Pipestone asked Teal Blake to create a design for them in 2005, they asked him to come up with a pattern that had a cowgirl as its subject. Their timing was perfect. Women have become increasingly visible as full counterparts to men in nearly every aspect of ranch life. Although they helped shape the frontier West as much as they take part in it today, few dinnerware artists had chosen to commemorate them until recently. Pipestone owner/design director Kathleen Kindig wasn't just keeping up with the times—she was setting a trend, one where women take the lead. In terms of design, she asked Teal for one color, simplifying the production process. They chose a timeless, sophisticated burgundy glaze on a white clay body. Just one color meant that the design would rely heavily on positive and negative areas to bring it to life. Blake came up with his distinctive pattern of a girl on a bronco, braids flying, and made it a classic. He adorned it with a tipi border and made each plate different, so the entire grouping tells a story.

Teal Blake. (Courtesy Tona Blake)

"Too Many Chiefs," watercolor by Teal Blake, an artist who knows the West.

"The overall look of the girl on the plate" explained Blake, "was referenced from old photos that my mother has of Fanny Sperry Steele, who was a lady bronc rider. I was able to meet her when she was ninety-two, and I

was probably five or six years old. My mother interviewed her for months to write a book about her. Fanny gave us tons of photos, all with a braid in her hair and riding a bronc. Her pictures are in the Cowboy Hall of Fame Rodeo Museum today in Colorado Springs, and

Top: Fanny Sperry Steele was the inspiration for this group, "Prairie Rose" designed by Teal Blake for Pipestone. (Photo by Lindsay Allen)
Left: Fanny Sperry Steele—an inspirational woman who could ride broncs as well as any man. (Courtesy National Cowgirl Museum)

my father has done a sculpture of her, as well, that's also there. The triangles are tipis, something that Pipestone had wanted. I believe we had tried barbed wire a few times, but that's been done so much. There are a few things I would change, looking back at the design now—I was fairly young when I did it—but I guess we're always the worst critic of our own work. I've come a long way since then."

"In honor of all the Western women who worked, played, and competed right along with their cowboy counterparts. On the ranch or in a rodeo, the Prairie Roses of their generation have always brought along color and romance wherever they rode."
—**K. Kindig,** Pipestone China

Teal is the great grandson of Samuel Coke Blake, one of the founding breeders of the American Quarter Horse. As did his great grandfather, he raises and shows quarter horses. They're a big part of his life, especially in his artwork. Teal lives in Wutherford, Texas, where he carries out commissions for many Western companies and private collectors.

Following in the footsteps of a father who's an established artist (Buckeye Blake), the younger Blake has already made a distinctive mark of his own. He was recently named one of the four Top Young Artists to Watch by *Western Horseman,* and it's certain that his design for this charming set of china will make it a collector's item ahead of its time. "Prairie Rose" captures a new sense of freedom expressed in a clean, bold contemporary rendition of a legendary cowgirl.

Triple Creek Products

2005–Current

Finding a consumer need and filling it seems to be the talent of successful manufacturers, and Triple Creek Products of Dallas, Texas, is no exception. Founded in 2005, the company's talented design team headed by Jeanie Edgar devotes their time to creating highly decorative rustic and Western inspired tabletop and wall décor. Designed in the U.S.A. but made offshore, the line is targeted for the residential user.

Top: "Andiron," sophisticated and timeless, a cross-over design. Modern and Western at the same time. (Courtesy Triple Creek)
Right: "Vintage," Triple Creek's version of the buckaroo on stoneware. Note how the plate mimics granite ware, but it's real china. (Place setting courtesy Cripple Creek)

Left: Andiron platter—simple and decorative (Platter courtesy Triple Creek)
Below: "Giddy Up," Melamine that looks like china. (Plate courtesy Triple Creek)

Triple Creek has captured a special feel in their Old West stoneware collection titled "Vintage," glazed in gray and brown and designed to resemble aged enamel over metal, with worn and chipped edges, an illusion created by the clever glaze application. The center motif of the bronco and rider is an exclusive design by Texas artist Teal Blake. Something about the feel of this image harks back to the *charro,* or Hispanic tradition, notably the wide sombrero-style hat.

The same bronc rider motif shows up on a fun and practical Melamine group known as the "Giddy Up" collection, perfect for picnics, trail rides, or cookouts—wherever unbreakable dinnerware is needed. This tableware is good-looking enough to be used at home as well, with a subtle matt finish that resembles crockery. The real triumph in tableware in their collection is their durable, everyday ironstone collection called "Andiron," clearly a contemporary solution for that back-at-the-ranch atmosphere. Clean, bold, and decidedly urban, the mix of the Texas Lone Star with the upturned horseshoes in rich colors of teal blue, sage, rust, and tobacco make this collection every urban cowgirl's choice. Triple Creek breaks new ground in taking the Western-themed genre into modern designer tableware with easy to use, trend-setting colors, and pieces that layer beautifully or mix and match.

Manufacturers of other unique serving bowls and home décor accent pieces, Triple Creek's take on Western-themed dinnerware might be a sign of things to come—transitional designs that keep the spirit of the West alive, interpreted in fresh new ways.

Rivers Edge Products
1997–Current

One of the best things about the Western home decor industry is the group of independent firms who are committed to interpreting the West *their* way. Rivers Edge Products in Saint Clair, Missouri, is one that has definitely carved out a niche for themselves, creating vintage and modern-era Lodge, Western, and Rustic style reproductions and novelties. Western retailers around the country sell their diverse lines of wall décor, accessories, and more recently—tableware.

Although the company has been around since 1997, their stoneware dinnerware set wasn't launched until 2008. The set features an image called "Learning the Ropes" by Randy Jay Braun. It's a simple statement about cowboy life—a transfer photo image of a cowboy and his son, each holding a lariat on a distressed China plate, clearly designed to mimic graniteware with its chipped edges.

The company's first entry into the tabletop category, the design is a good reminder that it's often the little things in life, especially the tender moments, which we cherish most. The charming photo came straight out of popular culture—off the Internet—as licensed stock photography. Rivers Edge Products felt that it had just what they were looking for—simplicity, sentiment, and timelessness. The sepia coloration of the photo adds to the collection's ambiance.

This combination of modern-day photography and Internet distribution is marketing a synthesis that often happens today—no matter that the piece is intended to resemble a vintage artifact. That's what makes it special and fun. Once retired, this four-piece place setting in any of its variations will rank as a definite collectible.

"Learning the Ropes" by Rivers Edge, a 4-piece place setting. Remarkable how a photograph can evoke a time and place and a lot of sentiment.

Pendleton Woolen Mills and Pendleton Dinnerware

2000–Current

The name Pendleton has a mystique all its own in the annals of Western products. The company's famous woolen blankets are known the world over and reflect a century of commitment to the weaver's art and to Native Americans in Pendleton, Oregon, where the woolen mill that first opened in 1909 still operates today.

All images this page: An American company with a great history and proud tradition. (Courtesy Pendleton Woolen Mills)

The company's earliest history began in 1863, when Thomas Kay came from England to the Oregon country to open a woolen mill in the Willamette Valley. Kay was a master craftsman at weaving cloth, and he passed his skills on to his daughter and three grandsons. It was the grandsons, Clarence, Roy, and Chauncey Bishop, who relocated to the community of Pendleton, in the Blue Mountain region of Oregon's Columbia Plateau, where they began weaving blankets for the local tribes. Today those blankets are the centerpiece of a unique American heritage, an index to tribal stories and symbols, and a colorful tableau that, individually, are works of art in their own right.

Oregon's Native American community consists of several different tribes who share the region and many traditions. A rough estimate is some 50,000 tribal members in all thirty-six counties of Oregon. Predominant among them are the tribes of Umatilla, the Burns Paiute, Tribe of Warm Springs, Grande Ronde, Coquille, Coos, Klamath, and Cow Creek band of Umpqua.

Pendleton "Round-Up" Collection

"The tradition began in 1909 with the opening of our mill in the heart of Pendleton, Oregon. A year later, and not more than a few steps down the road, the Pendleton Round-Up held its first rodeo. Like brothers, we've grown up together ever since.

We've come a long way in a hundred years, but we've held true to upholding the Western way of life. And today we celebrate that century of commitment with the Pendleton "Round-Up" collection, a line of apparel and home products reflecting the grit and integrity that made life out West possible."

—www.pendleton-usa.com

The famed Pendleton Round-Up, which will celebrate its 100th year in 2010, puts on one of the country's finest rodeos each September with full Native American participation. The tribes have been the most important customers of Pendleton's blanket production. Not only did the blankets provide warmth, but they were prized as trade items and often used as wedding gifts or ways to mark rites of passage.

Back in the early days of the company, staff member Joe Rawnsley, an expert on the Jacquard loom, studied the tribes of northeastern Oregon. Joe would go for months at a time to live

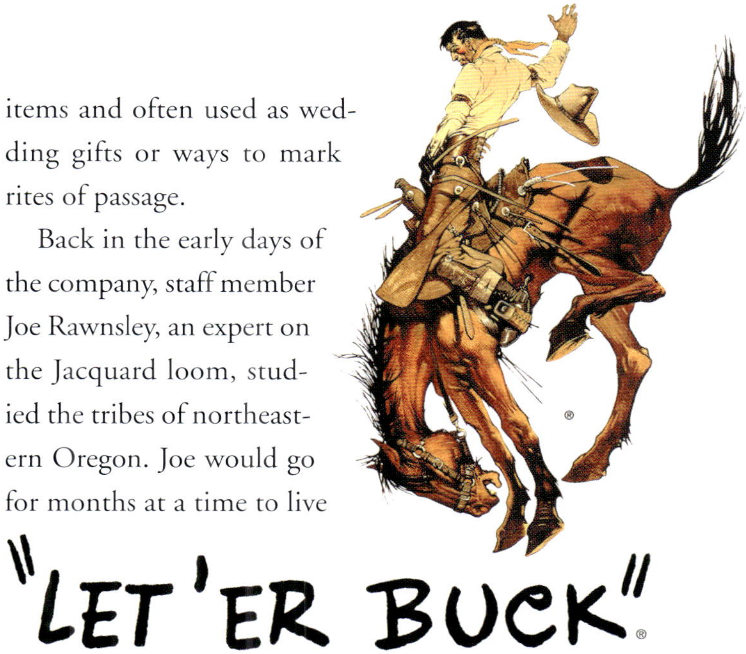

"LET 'ER BUCK"®

Commemorative design to celebrate the Pendleton Round-Up Rodeo's 100th Anniversary. A keepsake as well as a new look for the ranch house table.

with tribes to work on designs and learn their needs in order to help develop patterns they would want, with their preferences for color and design. He interpreted those elements into woolen blankets using then-modern technologies that could execute color and design even better than traditional weaving methods. He later studied tribes of the Southwest as well, developing ideas for designs for them. These blankets are sold via Pendleton stores throughout the country. An exclusive set of blanket designs benefits the Native American College Fund to help advance higher education for tribes in all areas.

With the popularity of the blanket patterns, it seemed inevitable that these exceptional designs would find their way to other applications. First came ceramic coffee mugs, and later two patterns of dinnerware, "Ranch House" and "Lakota," brilliant in color and design, both full place settings with stunning accessories. Earlier patterns of dinnerware, "Harding" and "Rock Art," were in the line for several years previously. Dishes are a marvelous way of adding ambiance to anyone's home, and although the product is manufactured offshore, the integrity of the designs is all-American.

The tabletop category is an important one that puts the Pendleton brand front and center for a new audience. The forthcoming occasion of Pendleton's 100th anniversary seemed an opportune time to create a commemorative earthenware series with the famed "Let 'Er Buck" logo, originally designed back in 1926 by Wallace Smith. The result is a perfect complement of old and new elements—the bronco and cowboy are framed by a simple dark brown border and stars. Uncluttered and "Old West" in feeling, the dinnerware seems the perfect accessory to keep the Round-Up spirit alive all year long.

"Ranch House" collection: inspired by the American Indian, a festive set in red and turquoise. Covered chip'n'dip server is a house favorite here.
Opposite: Lakota dinnerware, striking in indigo, brown, and white with faux basketry detail. A triumph that's both traditional and modern.

The first venture of Native American designs by Pendleton for tableware. The mugs are still best sellers.

Greystone Abbott

1999–Current

Although many ceramists are at work in America today creating quality handmade art pottery, few have dedicated themselves to creating functional ware celebrating their culture.

Meet Greystone Abbott, a registered Native American artist, a member of the Cherokee Confederacy of Georgia Bird Clan. A full-time professional potter since 1999, her work is hand-thrown and hand-painted, adorned with her original designs. Her dinnerware is made of a pottery clay body with additional grog for a stronger workable throw. Dinner sets include a dinner plate, salad plate, and a footed bowl. Greystone likes to let the customer mix and match designs, creating a totally customized look. There's often a proverb in the bottom of the bowls, so when the bowl is emptied, there's a reward at the end. The artist's favorite set has dream horses and proverbs on each bowl.

"Serve a salad, read a bowl," she adds. "I like to let the customer have a say in the creation process. It makes it more personal and they get what they want." The finished product is microwave, oven and dishwasher safe.

"I devote my time, energy, and soul into my earth walk as an artist having moved recently from Southern Utah to Colorado. I create usable art that is unique and beautiful and feel truly blessed to have been given this opportunity to create what I see in my mind's eye. I throw from my soul, inspired by my surrounding, and thank the Great Spirit daily for being able to do something I truly love—create."
—Greystone Abbott

"My Cherokee Choctaw heritage plays a big roll in the designs for my creations," the artist continued. "Creating has been a journey of self-discovery, listening to the clay and creating what's in my mind's eye."

Obviously, that creation is somewhere between the heritage of her people and a new and clear vision of something else, something strong and vibrant, alive with color and full of feeling. These bold platters are just the beginning of entire dinner sets in the designs shown. Custom orders have been shipped to clients across the United States. Each one is signed and titled by the artist.

Both a storyteller and an artist whose work transcends the narrative, Greystone Abbott offers a unique alternative to mass-produced ware. She has

"Two Sisters." Elegant and bold brush work. Understated simplicity makes this design work so very well. (Plate courtesy Greystone Abbott)

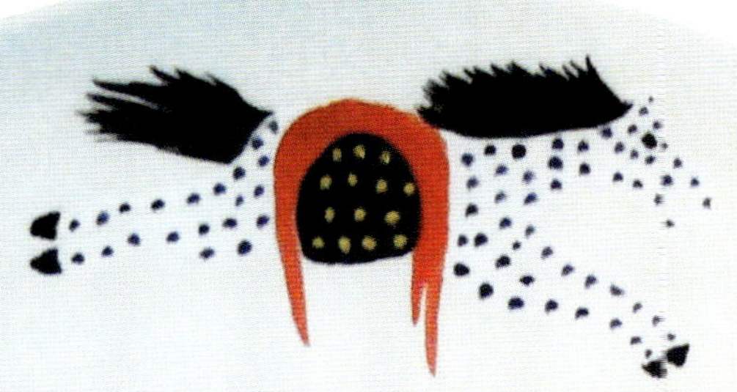

received numerous awards for her artwork and has participated in many exhibitions across the West, as well as at the Cherokee Heritage Center in Oklahoma and the VSA Arts Exhibit in Washington D.C. She is carried by Wild Spirit Gallery in Pagosa Springs, Colorado, where she makes her home.

Above: "Dream Horses," Oversize dinner plate or platter—mystical and bright, a wonderful play of line and color on white glaze. (Plate courtesy Greystone Abbott)
Right: "Wild Spirit," a strong and compelling gathering of horses on a highly decorative oversize plate. (Plate courtesy Greystone Abbott)

Tomorrow's West

We live in a visual world—clouds passing, patches of grass in greens and browns, sun dappling the earth. Fences bisecting the land. The world is an ever changing landscape of pattern, line, and color. Whether you're driving across America on Route 66, cantering through the sage and mesquite on the back of a horse, or soaring over the land by air, pattern defines our view. The West is a patchwork of mountains and sky, texture and color.

To the credit of a select few of today's dinnerware designers, the West has been reduced to its most essential elements. How remarkable that from those literal days of illustration where we were led, one line, one drawing at a time, into the landscape and lifestyle by image or symbol, we are now simply reminded that the West is here, a familiar palette and repetition of patterns understood by us all. Those in tune know the secret language of design. The visual West speaks to us in the simplest of terms.

Top: Clouds float through the endless sky of the Rocky Mountain West. Just looking up provides endless inspiration. Devil's Thumb Ranch, Tabernash, Colorado.

Above: Black and white cowhide china is a clever spin on the ultimate Western pattern. It adds a crisp look to any table, especially against colorful linens. Manufacturer Nick and Nora, a New York company in the giftware business since the 1980s, made the plate, available in dinner or salad size. The handsome cup, with a bucking bronco on one side and brands on the interior, is by Vandor, 1991. Don't they match well?

Gibson China

1980–Current

Gibson China is one of the world's largest manufacturers of packaged dinnerware sets sold at the mass-market level. With corporate headquarters in San Francisco, they're a family business committed to overseas production and national distribution. With all their variety, the West is a category not forgotten. Their understated pattern "American Cowboy" is merely a hint at the lifestyle—a denim fabric imprint on clay, glazed a subtle shade of blue (also done in red). This simple texture pattern says it all.

With the ribbed mark of the potter's wheel, this mass-produced ware looks completely handmade. Colored in a chambray blue, its surface evokes denim. "Urban Cowboy" by Gibson International. Cornflakes not included. (Courtesy Gibson)

Formations (Clay Art)

1980–Current

As chance would have it, my inquires into this product line inspired someone at Formations (owners of Clay Art) to notify former designer Timothy Matt of my interest in his pattern "Rodeo." Matt was once a designer for Clay Art, a long-established, California-based company in San Francisco, and had a wonderful feel for the essential West. The company employs in-house designers and produces in China with national distribution.

Clay Art's director was Karen Frankhausen, who confirms that the company was founded thirty years ago and still sells to many distribution channels—independents, department stores, catalogs, clubs, grocery stores, etc.

Texas

1896 *Platter*
UPC 0-98598 018965

1897 *Dip Bowls (Set of four)*
UPC 0-98598 018972

Western Plains

1930 *Platter*
UPC 0-98598 019306

1932 *Dinner Plate*
UPC 0-98598 019320

1953 *Mug*
UPC 0-98598 019351

1933 *Appetizer Plate*
UPC 0-98598 019337

1934 *Soup Bowl*
UPC 0-98598 019344

1931 *Dip Bowls (Set of four)*
UPC 0-98598 019313

© 2006 CLAY ART, INC. • 239 UTAH AVENUE • SOUTH SAN FRANCISCO, CA • 94080 • PHONE: (800) 252-9555 • EMAIL: INFO@CLAYART.NET

Reprint of catalog page from Clay Art, year 2000, featuring "Western Plains" dinnerware and "Texas" snack set.

"We create Western-themed dinnerware patterns at the request of our accounts," explained Karen, "mostly in Texas and the Southwest. The three-piece 'Western Plains' collection with the silhouetted cowboys was a best seller for us, designed originally by Jarv Falkard."

The warm caramel-glazed dinnerware group shown here was found on the shelves of a Denver discount chain store. The product, designed by Timothy Matt, had been titled "Tapestry" (in the backstamp) by someone overseas or in marketing who obviously didn't know what they were looking at. Nothing to my eye could be more Western, but then not everyone keeps a Western saddle in their bedroom either.

Matt, who once worked for West Coast producer Pacific Rim, had been recruited by Clay Art as a designer. After leaving their employ, he moved on to Caffco International, a manufacturing specialty giant. He was delighted to learn about the inclusion of his design in this book and asked if I knew that there was also a cookie jar, one shaped like a giant barrel with a cowboy hat on the lid. He was surprised to learn about the name change, reminding me that it was originally called "Rodeo!"

Clay Art also produced the intriguing dinner plate and mug titled "Western Plains," sometime during the latter 2000s. The seller said it came from Target, America's great equalizer, the place with something for everybody. I never imaged to find a plate like this there, however. Proof enough that the cowboy is back, waiting to be found, even between Aisles B and C.

Top left: "Rodeo" was an original design by Timothy Matt (now called "Tapestry" as the back stamp indicates), created for Clay Art. The embossed, carved leather pattern look (made in the mold) creates a fanciful tooled leather-like surface. It also comes in an olive green glaze. Certainly a Western setting for our times. (Photo by Lindsay Allen)
Left: Clay Art created a bold statement with "Western Plains," an iconic figure and handsome companion pieces in a rich reddish brown glaze.

CHAPTER 18

Life After the First Crack or Chip

Western Vintage Revival

And so it goes. Seventy years and counting. Inevitably, dinnerware succumbs to the travails of everyday life. Trends come and go, fashions wane, and the most popular dinnerware patterns fade into obscurity. Restaurants close, manufacturers shutter their doors. Sometimes vintage family heirloom dinner sets that have been stored away are taken out for use, and then—the inevitable happens. A chip here. A crack there. A plate breaks in the handling. Bit by bit, collections dwindle and many of us are left with mere remnants—a few reminders of the graceful tables we shared as kids. What then?

One enterprising artist named Jacqueline Smiley has managed to find the perfect way of preserving and transforming the vestiges of tablewares past. Her company, Vintage Revival and its Western division, now celebrating its twentieth year in business, is testament to the creativity and imagination needed for recycling ceramic dinnerware of all types, not just Western.

Disaster—even the most beloved china comes to this end. Don't throw it away.

Jacqueline has created a unique way of preserving the best of what was, searching out the most loved motifs, transfers, or details that can be wrapped in sterling silver and re-presented in a whole new way as art-to-wear. Her stunning inventory of necklaces, pendants, bracelets,

Above: There's hope in sight. China pieces can be effective elements for a new start. Or you can cut them up, like this, if you have the courage to. (Courtesy Vintage Revival)
Top Right: Pendant–It's amazing how a beautiful detail comes to life in the right setting. All it takes is great skill and an artistic eye. (Courtesy Western Vintage Revival)
Right: These jewelry designs can make an outfit. All you need is a black dress and a great pair of boots. (Courtesy Western Vintage Revival)

Above: There's more to these designs than you think. Jacqueline's team uses found objects, photos, and even recycled old sterling silverware. (Courtesy Vintage Revival)
Left: Jacqueline Smiley. (Courtesy Vintage Revival)

and earrings start their journey into our lives from a humble workshop in Altus, Okalahoma, where a series of loving hands cut, shape, and encase the mementos into their new existence. Combined with pearls, antique buttons, silver, and semi-precious jewels, as well as charms and miniature novelty items, found objects, silver flatware, miniature toys, and, of course, china bits.

The designs are attractive and intriguing. From a single silver-wrapped charm to a many-tiered necklace, each piece is more exceptional than the next. *Finally,* there's life after death for a dinner plate. Porcelain, pottery, and china may break, but this jewelry might last forever.

Jacqueline and her partners Lori and Chris Morris are the masterminds behind every piece, envisioning the final combination and theme that makes the company's work so successful. Originally trained in fashion and marketing, Jacqueline is a natural designer with a keen eye for creating the ensembles—various pieces including bracelets and earrings. A completely remodeled auto shop houses a cutting room with four stations for cutting and grinding, (complete with vacuums for absorbing all the dust) and a silver-smithing studio, a kitchen, and an office area for assembling and distribution, as well as a dust-free space for photography.

"In the beginning, I was originally inspired by Ming china pieces that I had seen at antique shows years ago made into pendants, or set into pill box covers," said Smiley. "Some made beautiful medallions. That was my inspiration. What I had seen, however, were all blue and white porcelain, and I was determined to seek out more colorful ware. In the beginning, we used solder to wrap the fragments, like stained-glass makers do. Then, about six years ago, we switched to sterling silver. That made all the difference."

From its humble start in Lancaster County, Pennsylvania, in 1990, Western Vintage Revival is now known nationwide for its spectacular jewelry designs, sought after by collectors and fans of dinnerware and the West.

"We really like to show our work directly to the customer," the artist continued. "So we do three major rodeos a year—in Houston, Texas; at the National Finals Rodeo in Las Vegas, Nevada; and at Wyoming

I don't know which way I like this dinnerware detail more—on the table or as a necklace. (Courtesy Vintage Revival)

Home, a retailer in Cheyenne, Wyoming, during Frontier Days. This year will be our third year as invitees to the Western Design Conference, as well, one of the most prestigious juried exhibitions in the country. We've been honored to have placed in the 'Jewelry' category with high distinction. We also do one large outdoor show, Mountain Heritage, at Harpers Ferry, West Virginia, a community dear to my heart, where many of our collectors have been our customers for more than twenty years."

A visit to the studio and home of Smiley uncovers what's important to this unusual talent. Jacqueline is an avid collector of antiques and Americana, including toys and furniture. Her Oklahoma family roots go all the way back to 1886, before the Oklahoma Land Rush, and she has all the documents to prove it. With this kind of inheritance and grounding in America's past, it's no wonder she's become the steward of broken and retired plates

A celebration of the West in silver and porcelain, this image of a bronc rider saved from a plate design is surrounded by Western silver charms. Note matching earrings with cowboy hats.

that find their way to her workshop. Vintage Western china, among other patterns, shall surely be preserved for a brighter future.

New dinnerware designers will surface every decade, and new interpretations of the West will shine. The next generation of motifs will surely grace the faces of pottery, porcelain, stoneware, and ironware. There's no telling what the future Western stories will be or how they will be told, but here's hoping that all of them can be preserved in some equally distinguished way.

Top left: Bad to the Bone—pistol-inspired jewelry combining dinnerware art and silver charms.
Top right: Vintage miniature Japanese ceramic figurine. The cowboy has been sawed in half and covered with silver on the back. Matching cowgirl, of course.
Lower Right: Belt buckle created from Hartstone's "Sky Ranch" dinnerware, green glaze on white—a stunning souvenir of the West.

CHAPTER 19

The Future of Western Dinnerware

Happy Trails to You

This chapter marks the end of a journey, the exploration of a genre that appeared to have a beginning, but apparently no end. As long as there are cowboys, there will be products to celebrate them. As long as people dine together, there will be new tableware to enjoy.

The last two decades saw the renaissance of Western-themed china. A fresh new crop of manufacturers has surfaced with new ideas, and the determination to spread the gospel that our homegrown cowboy culture is still alive and well and always will be.

Just think—over four hundred rodeos nationwide occur on the Fourth of July. Country Western and Rock 'n' Roll musicians in Los Angeles, Austin, Nashville, and New York alike can be spotted in cowboy boots and Western shirts, and just about every metropolitan city in this

By Storyteller Arts of Arizona, one of two companion snack bowls matching the large platter that closes our story (page 232). How clever that the loop the young cowboy is throwing encircles him on the rim of the bowl. A cheerful reminder of the roper's art, learned early by young cowpokes for fun. (One of the few depictions of a cowboy with no hat.)

Vintage planter. Unmarked piece of American art pottery, possibly McCoy or Hall. Whatever it is, it's a reminder of the courage that brought us West.

country has its hidden cowboy bar or honky-tonk. Denver has its Grizzly Rose, Fort Worth has Billy Bob's, and you can always have some fun in New York City at Cowgirl's in Manhattan. From Miami to San Francisco, across the urban range, you can eat barbecue or buffalo, buy a pair of hand-tooled boots, or find a dance bar where you can do the two-step, if you just know where to look.

According to Bob Boze Bell, publisher of *True West* magazine, the revival of interest in all things Western is more than underway. "Pound for pound," said Bell, in the August 2009 issue of *True West,* "more Western entertainment exists today than ever before. We have more Western artists, more Western poets, more Western singers, more Western music festivals, more Indian Pow Wows, more Western writers, more historical re-enactors, more Western books (many printed in England!), and yes, more Westerns on TV. Even in the so-called golden era of TV Westerns in the 1950s–60s, perhaps 26–30 shows ran in a week's time. Today we have the Westerns Channel, airing Western movies and TV shows 24/7. And with TMC and AMC and other channels often airing classic Westerns, as well as the production of special DVD sets, the bottom line is—Western enthusiasts have plenty of choices."

Today, as in the last century, visitors from abroad who dream of coming to America still put the West on the top of their agenda, not only to experience our national parks, but to see and experience historic towns and cities. They want to see our big skies, our canyons, mountains, and deserts, our wildlife, and especially cowboys and Indians.

In their own humble way, dinnerware artists and manufacturers are bringing you that West. Their artwork is unpretentious and unassuming. It's designed to whet your appetite for food *and* experience, to carry you back and transport you away. I'm hoping this excursion through their history and these products was worth your while. I apologize for excluding something that you have, and I missed, or that I didn't even know about. I will continue to collect for a long time to come.

I hope I've shown you something new. I can only tell you that if you own it now, hang on to it. It's probably more valuable than you think. Don't count on me for that validation, for this book was never intended to be a price guide—there are plenty of those and they're updated often. My goal was to give you context. If I've been successful, you'll never look at your cowboy dinnerware the same way again.

I encourage you to bring these delightful dishes into your life. Buy them in sets or separately, match them, stack them, and mix them up. Use them for social occasions or every day of the week. Just like the beloved cow camp chuck wagon chef, why not cook up a storm and invite all your friends. Put the coffee on, ring the dinner bell, and holler, "Come and get it!" Then, get out of the way.

This charming oversize platter is another house favorite. Purchased at Dillards, made by Story Teller Arts. This happy-go-lucky cowboy is a reminder that life is good and tomorrow will be even better.

Bibliography

Allen, Henry. *What It Felt Like: Living in the American Century,* Pantheon Books, New York, New York, 2000.

Aquila, Richard. *Wanted Dead or Alive: The American West in Popular Culture,* University of Illinois Press, Urbana, Illinois, 1996.

Bess, Phyllis and Tom Bess. *Frankoma and Other Oklahoma Potteries,* Schiffer Publishing, Atglen, Pennslyvania, 2000.

Biddle, Julian. *What Was Hot: A Rollercoaster Ride Through Six Decades of Pop Culture in America,* Citadel Press, New York, New York, 2002.

Brody, J. J. Mimbres Pottery: *Ancient Art of the American Southwest,* Hudson Hills Press, 1983.

Corey, Melinda. *Chronology of 20th-Century America,* Decades of American History, Facts on File, Inc., New York, 2005.

Conroy, Barbara. *Restaurant China: Identification & Value Guide for Restaurant, Airline, Ship & Railroad Dinnerware, Volume 1,* Collector Books, a division of Schroeder Publishing, Paducah, Kentucky, 1998.

____. *Restaurant China: Identification & Value Guide for Restaurant, Airline, Ship & Railroad Dinnerware, Volume 2,* Collector Books, a division of Schroeder Publishing, Paducah, Kentucky, 1999.

Cunningham, Jo. *Homer Laughlin China: 1940s and 1950s,* Schiffer Publishing, Atglen, Pennsylvania 2000.

____. *The Best of Collectible Dinnerware,* Schiffer Publishing, Atglen, Pennsylvania, 1999.

Dollen, B.L. and R.L. Dollen. *Red Wing Art Pottery,* Collector Books, a division of Schroeder Publishing, Paducah, Kentucky, 1998.

Etling, Kathy. *The Quotable Cowboy,* Lyons Press, Guilford, Connecticut, 2002.

Graffe, Steve, Susan Hallsten McGarry, Charles Rand, Richard Rattenbury, Donald Reeves, foreword by Chuck Schroeder. *A Western Legacy: The National Cowboy & Western Heritage Museum,* University of Oklahoma Press, Norman, Oklahoma, 2005.

Grattan, Virginia. *Mary Colter: Builder Upon the Earth,* 2nd Edition, Northland Press Flagstaff, Arizona, 1992.

Hall, Terry. *Cowboy Wisdom,* Modern Man Books/Warner Books, Clayton Vic, Australia, 1995.

Batchelor, John Calvin, and John Hamilton. *Thunder in the Dust: Great Shots from the Western Movies,* Workman Publishing, New York, New York, 1987.

Harle, Leslie and Susan Conder Harle. *Designer China: Fine Art of Ceramic Painting Made Simple,* Hearst Books, New York, New York, 1991.

Hassrick, Royal. *Cowboys and Indians: An Illustrated History,* Promontory Press, a division of A&W Promotional Book Corporation, New York, New York, 1976.

Hill, Anne Terry and Michael Bales. *Pendleton Round-Up at 100: Oregon's Legendary Rodeo,* Graphic Arts Books, Portland, Oregon, 2009.

Hilfiger, Tommy and George Lois. *Iconic America: A Roller Coaster Ride through the Eye-Popping Panorama of American Pop Culture,* Universe Publishing, a division of Rizzoli International. New York, New York, 2007.

Lucetti, Kathy. *Home on the Range: A Culinary History of the American West,* Villard, New York, New York, 1993.

Johnson, Michael L. *The New Westers: The West in Contemporary American Culture,* University Press of Kansas, Lawrence, Kansas, 1996.

Montana, Gladiola. *Never Ask a Man the Size of His Spread: A Cowgirl's Guide to Life,* Gibbs Smith Publishing, Salt Lake City, Utah, 1995.

Morris, Michele. *The Cowboy Life: A Saddlebag Guide for Dudes, Tenderfeet, and Cowpunchers Everywher*e, Fireside Books/Simon & Schuster, New York, New York, 1993.

Nelson, Maxine Feek. *Collectible Vernon Kilns,* Collector Books, a division of Schroeder Publishing, Paducah, Kentucky, 2003.

O'Byrne, Tim. *Cowboys and Buckaroos*: *Trade Secrets of a North American Icon, Western Horseman* magazine, Colorado Springs, Colorado, 2005.

Reed, Cleota, and Stan Skoczen. *Syracuse China,* Syracuse University Press, Syracuse, N.Y., 1997.

Schaut, Jim and Nancy Schaut. *Collecting the Old West*, Krause Publishing, Iola, Wisconsin, 1999.

Smith, Martin J. and Patrick J. Kiger. *Poplorica: A Popular History of Fads, Mavericks, Inventions, and Lore that Shaped Modern America,* Collins, New York, New York, 2004.

Snyder, Jeffrey. *McCoy Pottery: A Field Guide,* 3rd Edition, A Schiffer Book for Collectors, Schiffer Publishing, Atglen, Pennslyvania, 2002.

Stern, Jane and Michael Stern. *Way Out West,* Harper Perennial, New York, New York, 1993.

Venable, Charles. *China and Glass in America: From Tabletop to TV Tray,* Dallas Museum of Art, Abrams Publishing, New York, New York, 2001.

Warren, Holly George. *Cowboy: How Hollywood Invented the Wild West,* Reader's Digest International, Ivy Press Limited, East Sussex, United Kingdom, 2002.

Weil, Steven E. and Daniel DeWeese. *Western Shirts: A Classic American Fashion,* Gibbs Smith Publishing, Salt Lake City, Utah, 2004.

Index

Photo by Ellen Jaskol

THE WEST FOR ME has always been about horses, cowboys 'n cowgirls, and endearing memories. This book has been a special lens by which I could view them all again.

Here's hoping you enjoyed the ride.

—CORINNE J. BROWN